TRAILHEAD

THE DIRT ON ALL THINGS
TRAIL RUNNING

LISA JHUNG

ILLUSTRATIONS BY
CHARLIE LAYTON

VELO press

Boulder, Colorado

3002 Sterling Circle, Suite 100
Boulder, Colorado 80301-2338 USA
(303) 440-0601 Fax (303) 444-6788
E-mail velopress@competitorgroup.com

Distributed in the United States and Canada by Ingram Publisher Services

A Cataloging-in-Publication record for this book is available from the Library of Congress.
ISBN 978-1-937715-32-8

For information about purchasing VeloPress books,
please call (800) 811-4210, ext. 2138, or visit www.velopress.com.

Illustrations and cover design by Charlie Layton
Interior design by Vicki Hopewell and Erin Farrell

15 16 17 / 10 9 8 7 6 5 4 3 2 1

CONTENTS

Welcome to the Trail

Welcome to the trail.

If you've ever been outside, you know that simply standing on a natural surface can make a person happier. *Running on a trail—*dirt, grass, sand, and such—enhances the happiness and adds the benefits of becoming healthier, stronger, fitter . . . more joyful, even. It grounds you.

Luckily for us, trails are everywhere.

A "trail" is not defined by how steep it is, how far it climbs up a mountain, how treacherous the footing, or how many miles it spans. Trails can be completely flat, rolling, or downright mountainous. They can be in the wilderness, farmland, your neighborhood, or a city park.

And a "trail runner" has a broad definition, too. Speeding through the hills like a mountain goat makes you a trail runner. So does hopping on a smooth dirt path and moving your feet in some motion faster than a walking or hiking pace for a couple of miles. From newbies with still-pink toenails to wily veterans who depend on pedicures for normalcy, from dedicated road runners with a longing for nature and a more forgiving surface to ultrarunners accustomed to hallucinations and gastrointestinal distress, you are all trail runners, and this book is for you.

By providing a no-nonsense (okay, a little nonsense) visual reference to everything there is to know about trail running—what

to do when encountering a bear, or (sometimes) worse, a charging mountain biker or cantankerous hiker; what to wear to embrace the elements; how to relieve yourself on the trail without embarrassing yourself or those around you; or how to get faster or go farther—this book will help you thrive.

What is a trail?

trail \trāl\ *n. (pl. -s)* 1. An unpaved path that goes somewhere.

A TRAIL	NOT A TRAIL
Dirt path	Concrete path
Rocky path	Asphalt road
Mossy path	Sidewalk
Rooty path	Freeway
Dirt road	Treadmill
Gravel path	Track
Gravel road	Bouncy house
Rail trail converted to dirt path	Target store (no matter how
Sandy beach	many aisles you cover)
Grassy field	

The "unpaved path" refers to any surface not covered in concrete, asphalt, bricks, or tiles. The "goes somewhere" component eliminates a treadmill, grassy sports field, or rubber track. While those venues confer some of the same physical and mental benefits as running on a trail, the "goes somewhere" bit of the definition is what gives you a sense of adventure.

ADVENTURE: A SLIDING SCALE

There is a sense of adventure, there is an actual adventure, and then there is an epic adventure. Trail running can sometimes be all three.

Sense of adventure. A feeling of excitement when you set out on your run, all but guaranteed on even the mellowest of trails. *I'm so ready to do this!*

Actual adventure. A trail run offering a sense of exploration, discovery, and even a bit of apprehension. *This is exciting! Can I do this?*

Epic adventure. A trail run rich with excitement, challenge, endurance, and possibly crazy weather conditions. Epic adventures vary, but they all end with the same thought: *That was awesome! I did this!*

Adventures are out there for the taking. But not every run (or any run) has to be epic to be great. Some days you may want to just get outside and take it mellow and easy on a familiar nearby path. Regardless of where your runs fall on the sliding scale of adventure, if you want to keep your off-road running fun and safe, this book will help you plan runs wisely.

How to use this book

The 12 chapters in this book fall into six categories, each examining trail running from a different angle. Feel free to read every page twice, quote it to your running mates, and get a great kick out of the illustrations. Heck, buy a copy for each of your friends. However, there is no need to read *Trailhead* in order, from beginning to end. Flip through each chapter as needed. Strict order is as important in this book as it is in trail running, which is to say not very.

➡ WHY. Wherein we discuss what trail running does for your body and your mind.

➡ HOW. These chapters answer questions about where to go and what you need to trail run. They also discuss how to handle weather, what to wear, and how to fuel up.

➡ SAFETY. These chapters spell out what to do if you encounter animals on your run. And they talk about basic first aid.

➡ ETIQUETTE. This chapter discusses good behaviors for multiuse trails, including who has the right of way. It also teaches about the socially and environmentally acceptable ways to relieve yourself during a run. And ways to preserve our beloved trails.

⇒ COMPANY: This chapter weighs the pros and cons of running by yourself; with friends; with dogs, horses, or burros (for real).

⇒ HOW, PART II: These chapters delve into training for trail running, including strengthening exercises, workouts, and tips on technique to make you stronger and faster. They also offer some guidance on trail racing.

CHAPTER 1

Why: Your Body

Running on trails does a body good. Thanks to varied terrain and softer natural surfaces underfoot, running on trails can both improve your overall fitness and be more forgiving to your body than road running.

Nice bod

A fit physique may not be your main reason to head out for a run on trails, but it's not a bad side effect. Running on variable surfaces, such as trails riddled with rocks or roots—or even on smooth, twisty singletrack—forces your body to use stabilizing muscles (hello, core) and strengthen connective tissues (ligaments and tendons) that don't normally get recruited on road runs. And running hilly terrain on trails builds leg strength—working quads, calves, and gluteal muscles more than running on flats.

The Trail Runner's Leg

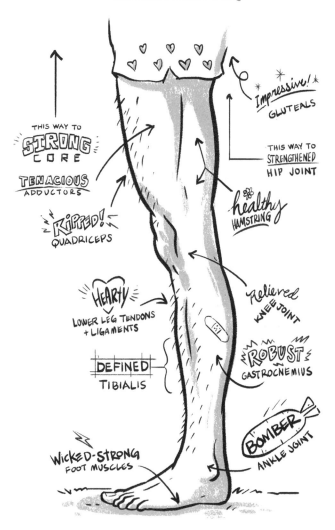

THIS WAY TO **STRONG** CORE

TENACIOUS ADDUCTORS

RIPPED! QUADRICEPS

HEARTY LOWER LEG TENDONS + LIGAMENTS

DEFINED TIBIALIS

WICKED-STRONG FOOT MUSCLES

Impressive! GLUTEALS

THIS WAY TO **STRENGTHENED** HIP JOINT

healthy HAMSTRING

Relieved KNEE JOINT

ROBUST GASTROCNEMIUS

BOMBER ANKLE JOINT

Plus, research shows that trail running can burn up to 10 percent more calories than running on a road or track for the same time or distance.

Better balance

The varied terrain of trails engages small, intrinsic muscles situated deep within our bodies for balance, improving coordination by teaching us proprioception.

proprioception \prō-prē-uh-ˈsep-shun\ *n.* 1. Awareness of the position of one's body, helpful to runners and all other living creatures.

Running trails has multiple benefits. Science says so!

- Studies show that walking on uneven terrain requires more energy than walking on smooth ground, engaging more muscle activity and metabolic expenditure. *If this applies to walking, just think how it applies to running.*

- Running trails—unstable ground, uphill/downhill, altitude— often strengthens balancing muscles, such as core muscles and small stabilizing muscles, normally not engaged in road running.

- Trail surfaces are softer than pavement and thus create lower overall impact and reduced pain while running.

- Running trails improves bone density that may help combat osteoporosis.

"Mechanically, trail running challenges athletes in all three planes of motion: sagittal (front/back), frontal (side/side), and transverse (rotational). This means there's a high degree of muscle control and strength, plus coordination and proprioception, required to trail run."

CHARLIE MERRILL, licensed physical therapist and competitive trail runner

Soft landing

Trails compress, or dampen, to varying degrees with every step. That means that each time your foot hits the ground on trail, the impact is less harsh than on pavement or concrete. This minimizes wear and tear on your body—the same kind of wear and tear caused by the repetitive motion of running on a hard surface, which can lead to a multitude of overuse injuries.

And the softer the surface, the more energy your body expends to rebound during your stride—a good thing. Running on very soft surfaces (such as deep sand) increases muscular strength and overall stamina.

"In the same way you go to the gym to get strong, running on changing terrain makes muscles, tendons and ligaments stronger. Compliant surfaces are great for muscles and joints because they store and return your energy. Running in the sand, which has a lot of dampening, works foot and calf muscles and burns a lot of energy. And running on uneven terrain makes your heart rate and overall energy cost go up."

DANIEL FERRIS, PHD, professor, School of Kinesiology, University of Michigan

Easy does it

Doing too much too soon can shock your body and cause injuries.

With any training program, easing into things is important. With trail running, gradually building up to more technical terrain will give your muscles, joints, ligaments, and tendons time to adjust and prepare them to become stronger than ever.

YOUR BODY HAS A LOT TO GAIN FROM TRAIL RUNNING.

If you're a road runner . . .	**You have:** Cardiovascular stamina, leg strength, good bone density
	You'll gain: Core strength, intrinsic muscle strength, balance, agility
If you're a hiker . . .	**You have:** Some cardiovascular stamina, some core strength, leg strength
	You'll gain: Increased cardiovascular stamina, increased core strength, increased leg strength, increased bone density from the impact of running, balance, agility
If you're a rock climber . . .	**You have:** Core strength, some cardiovascular stamina, leg strength, upper body strength
	You'll gain: Increased cardiovascular stamina, increased leg strength, increased bone density from the impact of running, balance, agility, faster access to climb sites
If you do yoga . . .	**You have:** Isometric leg strength (from holding poses), balance, flexibility
	You'll gain: Cardiovascular stamina, dynamic leg strength, improved bone density from the impact of running, counterstrengthening to your flexibility (shortening of muscles for power), agility, enjoyment of being outdoors
If you do Pilates . . .	**You have:** Core strength, muscular strength
	You'll gain: Cardiovascular stamina, increased muscular strength, increased bone density from the impact of running, a great way to apply your core strength, balance, agility, enjoyment of being outdoors

If you're a road cyclist . . .	**You have:** Cardiovascular stamina, leg strength (singular plane/circular)
	You'll gain: Core strength, dynamic leg strength, increased cardiovascular strength (your legs keep moving downhill), increased bone density from the impact of running, increased balance, increased agility
If you're a mountain biker . . .	**You have:** Cardiovascular stamina, leg strength (singular plane/circular), some core strength
	You'll gain: Increased core strength, dynamic leg strength, increased cardiovascular strength (your legs keep moving downhill), increased bone density from the impact of running, increased balance, increased agility, another perspective of the trails you love (and access to some you can't ride)
If you're a surfer, skier, or snowboarder . . .	**You have:** Some cardiovascular stamina, leg strength—mostly isometric from holding one position for long periods of time, balance, core strength, hand-eye-foot coordination
	You'll gain: Increased cardiovascular stamina, dynamic leg strength, increased bone density from the impact of running, increased core strength, improved balance and agility, faster access to waves and pow
If you're a Nordic skier . . .	**You have:** Cardiovascular stamina, core strength, leg strength, upper-body strength
	You'll gain: A way to train everything when the snow melts, increased bone density from the impact of running

If you do CrossFit . . .	**You have:** Muscular strength (mostly on two legs, not one at a time), core strength, short-intensity cardiovascular strength, agility
	You'll gain: Cardiovascular stamina, increased muscular strength (on one leg at a time), increased bone density from the impact of running, enjoyment of being outdoors
If you play ball sports . . .	**You have:** Some cardiovascular strength, muscular strength, core strength
	You'll gain: Increased and sustained cardiovascular stamina, increased muscular strength, mental break from team competition
If you're a swimmer . . .	**You have:** Cardiovascular stamina, core strength, upper-body strength
	You'll gain: Improved cardiovascular stamina, leg strength, increased core strength, increased bone density from the impact of running, balance, agility, a change of scenery from the bottom of the pool
If you're on the couch . . .	**You have:** A need to get off the couch
	You'll gain: Everything except weight

CHAPTER 2

Why: Your Mind

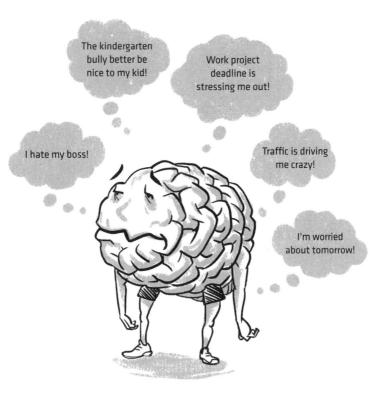

Your Brain Before a Trail Run

Your Brain After a Trail Run

Trail running goes beyond strengthening just your body. Runners know—and research supports—that it's also ridiculously good for your heart, mind, and soul.

Peace of mind

A run is powerful medicine. It can turn a bad mood into a good one, give you a new perspective on an old problem, and leave you feeling calm and in more control than before you started your run.

Add the benefits of being outside on a trail—with fresh air; the smell of trees and grass; and the sights, sounds, and sensation of nature underfoot—and you just may find yourself launched into a state of Zen. Or close.

Scientists have measured the benefits of exercise outdoors on our mental well-being. Here are some of the conclusive findings:

- Exercising in natural environments increases energy and creates greater feelings of revitalization and positive engagement.

- Exercising in natural environments decreases tension, confusion, anger, and depression.

- A high dose of negative ions combats depression. *Negative ions come out of trees . . . for free!*

- Bright light is effective for treatment of chronic depression and for mood improvement. *Guess what? There's a natural bright light available while running: the sun.*

Bright white light improves mood.

Sense of increased energy and vitality after exercising outdoors.

Negative ions combat depression.

- Participants in one study reported greater enjoyment and satisfaction with outdoor activity than with indoor exercise and declared a greater intent to repeat the activity. *Stick-to-it fitness bonus!*

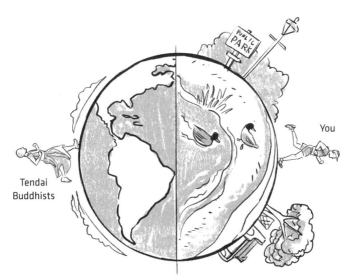

You

Tendai
Buddhists

Path to Enlightenment

Trail running and meditation have been linked for centuries.

For over 400 years, the Tendai Buddhists of Japan's Mount Hiei have run 18 to 32 miles either 100 or 200 days straight for 7 years, figuratively circling the globe on foot on a path to enlightenment.

Don't sweat it: To reap the benefits of melding mindfulness with movement, circling your local park may be all you need.

SAYS WHO

"Trail running can be a mini-vacation for the mind. For people who have a hard time being in the moment, are worried about the future or lamenting the past, trail running is a mental break."

DEAN HEBERT, mental game coach and author of *Coach, I Didn't Run Because . . .*

Running reinvigorated!

If you're a road runner, know that hitting the dirt can breathe new life into your weekly training. Occasional trail runs make you both a physically and a mentally stronger road runner. Those hills in your 10K won't seem so hard. And that storm that rolls in during your marathon? Your trail runner self laughs in the face of weather adversity.

Even if you are a dedicated road runner who thrives on a disciplined running regimen with measured times and distances, mixing things up by going off-road can break you out of a rut and bring you back refreshed.

Consider doing some of your long, slow distance training or your recovery days on a trail. You can also do speed work or other workouts on trails (see "Training: Mix It Up," page 221). Running on a different surface, with a change of scenery and less structure, can actually make you look forward to your next road run or track session.

CHAPTER 3

How: Where to Go

Trails, Trails, Everywhere

You don't have to live in a mountain town to be a trail runner. Trails exist in urban areas, suburban areas, rural farmlands, and coastal communities. In fact, there are over 60,000 miles of trails in the United States. You just need to know how to find them.

What's outside your door?

Suburban trails

Many suburban areas have dirt, wood-chipped, or gravel paths within town limits. These areas are popular for dog walkers, fitness walkers, bicyclists, and nature lovers and offer soft surfaces away from traffic. Some suburban areas also have dirt alleys and paths linking paved streets. Ask around, or go out and explore to find them.

Rural trails

Rural areas often offer plenty of open spaces and opportunities for exploring dirt and grass paths, some likely carved out by animals. Running on a dirt road or over hill and dale in quiet farmland provides a soft surface and pleasant bucolic views. *Note:* On dirt roads, run on the side of the road *against* traffic, and always stay aware of your surroundings. Car, truck, and tractor drivers may not be used to seeing runners on the sides of rural roads.

Horse trails

Horse trails can be found in rural areas, but they sometimes also twist through communities where residents who own horses like to ride. Some areas have extensive wood-chipped and dirt trails running throughout. *Note:* Some towns specify that their equestrian trails are for residents and riders only. Always be courteous to horses and their riders. For details on proper trail etiquette, see "Etiquette," page 164.

Urban trails

Even in major urban centers, you can find trails. San Francisco has great ribbons of smooth singletrack running through Golden Gate Park and the Presidio. New York City has trails winding through Central Park and Van Cortlandt Park. Most cities have trails within city limits and even more within a short drive.

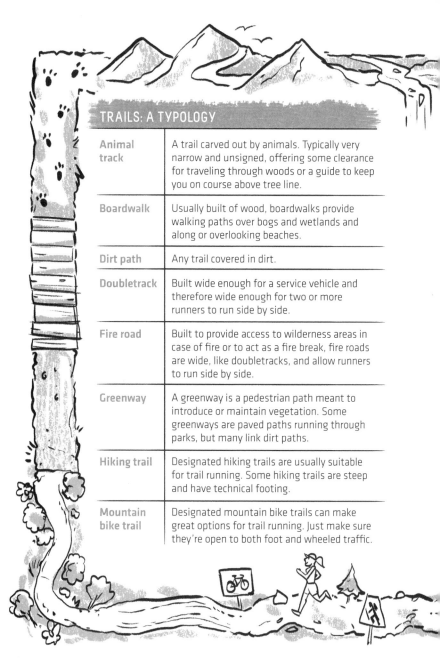

TRAILS: A TYPOLOGY

Animal track	A trail carved out by animals. Typically very narrow and unsigned, offering some clearance for traveling through woods or a guide to keep you on course above tree line.
Boardwalk	Usually built of wood, boardwalks provide walking paths over bogs and wetlands and along or overlooking beaches.
Dirt path	Any trail covered in dirt.
Doubletrack	Built wide enough for a service vehicle and therefore wide enough for two or more runners to run side by side.
Fire road	Built to provide access to wilderness areas in case of fire or to act as a fire break, fire roads are wide, like doubletracks, and allow runners to run side by side.
Greenway	A greenway is a pedestrian path meant to introduce or maintain vegetation. Some greenways are paved paths running through parks, but many link dirt paths.
Hiking trail	Designated hiking trails are usually suitable for trail running. Some hiking trails are steep and have technical footing.
Mountain bike trail	Designated mountain bike trails can make great options for trail running. Just make sure they're open to both foot and wheeled traffic.

Mountain trail	A trail in the mountains, typically characterized by ascending and descending, sometimes crossing creeks, often at a high altitude.
Rail trail	A trail converted from defunct railways to recreational use. While many rail trails are asphalt or concrete, some are crushed gravel, stone, or dirt.
Singletrack	A narrow path just wide enough for one trail user at a time.
Social trail	A trail carved out by humans such as hikers, runners, or bikers. Similar to an animal track in that it is a trail not planned by land managers. Using it can cause damage to an ecosystem.
Snowmobile trail	Snowmobile trails make great winter running paths because snowmobiles pack down fresh snow so it's harder, like hard-packed sand. Be aware of snowmobiles, and when you hear them, move to the side.
Snowshoe trail	Designated trails specifically for snowshoeing, mostly found at Nordic centers and/or alpine ski resorts.
System trail	A trail that has been designed, built, and managed with permission by the landowner or land manager.
Wood-chip trail	A trail covered in wood chips, usually found in city and suburban parks.

Beaches

Sandy beaches count as trails. Hard-packed sand is much easier to run on than soft sand. Check local tide charts for low tide; when the tide is the lowest, you'll have the largest area of hard-packed sand on which to run. On the other hand, soft, deep sand provides a fun, challenging workout and makes any runner stronger.

Mountain trails

Mountain towns usually have trails in every direction, which means a lot of choices, depending on your mood. Trails can head straight up a mountain for a leg- and lung-burning workout. Some cut across mountains, offering rolling terrain instead of major climbs. And some run along valley floors, providing a flat option with views of soaring peaks. In winter months, snowy trails packed down by snowmobiles and touring skis offer the ability to step into a pair of snowshoes and run wherever there's snow coverage. (See "Snowshoe Running: It's Easier Than You Think," page 63.)

Finding a trail

Trail running is all about exploring, but you have to know where to start. Luckily, finding an unpaved surface to run on is as easy as asking a buddy or typing a few words into an Internet search.

- **Ask a friend.** Where do your trail running friends like to go? If they don't know your running level, be specific about the type of trail or experience you're looking for. You don't want to end up on a steep, rocky mountain trail if you're better equipped for a flat, wide dirt path.

- **Inquire at a running or outdoor store.** People who work in running stores or outdoor stores are often passionate participants in the sports requiring the gear they sell. They are excellent resources for learning about trails in your area. Be specific about the type of trail you're looking for, and don't be afraid to ask a lot of questions about the trails they recommend.

- **Join a running club.** Your local running shop may host weekly runs. Or do an Internet search for "trail running club in [your town here]." Don't be intimidated by group runs. They are usually open to runners of all speeds and levels. Group runs are a great way to learn your way around the local trails, and there's a good chance you'll meet new friends who share your interest in exploring new trails. See "Joining a Running Group," page 191.

- **Search trail resources.** Check out a trail or hiking guidebook for your area, inquire at public land use agency offices, or search the Internet for "running trails (or "hiking trails") in [your town here]." Read trail descriptions closely for information about difficulty level and other details.

- **Reconnoiter.** Exploring your neighborhood on foot can unveil things heretofore unnoticed, including trails. You might be surprised to find dirt alleys, wood-chip walking paths, or short trails that lead to a whole network of longer trails.

Staying found

As you're exploring new trails, you don't want to get lost. Here's how to stay found:

- **Go with someone.** Running with someone who knows the trails is a surefire way to stay found. Unless, of course, your friend has a bad sense of direction . . . For added insurance, follow the tips below.

- **Read a map.** Ideally, you'll bring along a map of the trails on which you plan to run. Realistically, you may not. Study a map before heading out to give you an idea of the lay of the land—how long the trail is, where to turn around, etc.

- **Keep your bearings.** As you're running, pay attention to your surroundings. If you recall that you crossed a stream and took a hard left up a hill, you'll be better able to find your way back.

- **Carry your phone or other GPS device.** GPS-tracking devices, when they can detect a signal, can provide invaluable information to help you find your way back home if you do become lost.

- **Sign in:** Trail registries can be found at the trailheads of many remote trails. Signing in with your name, the date and time, your planned route, and when you expect to be back gives rangers valuable information should you get lost or injured.

TRAIL REGISTER SHEET

TRAIL NAME: _____

DATE	NAME	ACTIVITY	COMMENTS:
7/20	DAN FREEMAN	SPEED HIKING	CIRCUMNAVIGATING RESERVOIR
7-21	Sara Yoder	Hiking 14er	Summit by noon
7/21	Mark Eller	Running	Later, suckas!

Suit your mood

One of the greatest things about trails is the sheer variety available. What kind of run do you feel like doing? There's a trail for that. Some days you just want to go easy and turn your legs over along a smooth dirt path. Other days you may be in the mood for the rockiest, rootiest, hilliest trail around.

THE DIRT Some people lose themselves in thought better on mellow trails that don't require them to think about footing. Others get a mental break on trails that force them to focus on each step rather than on, say, the crazy situation at their job.

Here's how to find a trail that suits your experience level, training goal, or mood on any given day.

I want . . .

- **a flat and easy trail.** Seek out rail trails; paths where people walk their dogs or casually ride bikes; or nature trails in city, state, and national parks.

- **a hilly trail.** Seek out hiking or mountain trails. State, local, and federal public lands web sites often list trailheads.

- **a trail that's good for my dog, too.** Great trails for dogs include those that cross over or travel next to streams or lakes and are shaded. Hilly trails are great for dogs because their owners tend to slow the pace. Check local dog leash and tag laws before you go. (For more on running with dogs and other animals, see "Running with Human or Animal Friends," page 186.)

- **a sheltered trail.** To avoid wind, rain, snow, or harsh sun, check out singletrack trails in dense woods. The tree cover often shields the trail from the elements and provides shade on blistering summer days.

- **a challenging trail.** Seek out trails that hiking web sites rate "difficult" or mountain bike trails that web sites rate "difficult" or that are labeled with a black diamond. These may be steep, or they may be riddled with challenges such as rocks or other obstacles. Or run up the tallest natural feature in your town.

- **an epic trail.** Consider a run vacation and head to the mountains, the desert, the forest . . . somewhere remote or on your bucket list of must-do runs.

THE DIRT A mellow trail can be transformed into a challenging trail just by running it in foul weather or other difficult conditions—which can be both fun and rewarding.

CHAPTER 4

How: Gear

| What You Must Wear to Trail Run | What You Could Wear to Trail Run | What Totally Enhances a Trail Run |

Part of the beauty of trail running is its simplicity: You don't need a closet full of special gear to hit the trails. Have some shorts? A T-shirt? You're good to go. That said, wearing goods specifically designed for trail running will make you more comfortable on everything from mellow dirt paths to gnarly mountain scrambles.

Shoes

Gather up a group of trail runners, and soon enough the talk will turn to shoes. Minimal shoes. Maximal shoes. No shoes. Choices for footwear run the gamut from stiff and burly to super-cushed-out to thin-soled and form-fitting. The key is finding the shoe that works for you and your personal needs.

You can run on a trail in road running shoes. However, shoes specifically made for trail running are generally more stable, pro-tective, sure-footed, and durable than road running shoes.

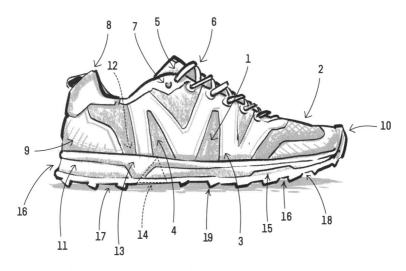

[1] Upper: The parts and materials that wrap around the top and sides of your foot.

[2] Closed mesh: Tighter-woven mesh than you'd find on a road running shoe, intended to keep out trail gunk.

[3] **Overlays:** Materials sewn or welded to the otherwise soft and flexible upper, meant to provide structure and stability. Trail shoes often have more overlays than do road running shoes.

[4] **Sidewall:** The side of the shoe surrounding your arch and the side of your foot. Trail shoes generally offer more sidewall protection than do road shoes.

[5] **Tongue:** The part of the upper that lies under the laces. The tongue of some trail running shoes is connected to the upper to help keep out debris.

[6] **Laces:** Stringy things that tie up your shoes. Some laces tighten and secure with one pull, eliminating the need to tie. (See "Tie One On," page 38.)

[7] **Eyelets:** The holes that the laces pass through.

[8] **Collar:** The opening in the upper where your foot enters the shoe. Usually padded for comfort, the amount of padding varies from shoe to shoe.

[9] **Heel counter:** A firm, plastic, cup-shaped piece often sandwiched between soft materials around the back of your heel, intended to provide stability and help your foot track straight with each step. Not found on all shoes.

[10] **Toe bumper:** Rubber or plastic on the front of the shoe meant to protect toes from getting stubbed on rocks and roots. Made of varying degrees of burliness, from soft rubber to hard plastic. Not found on all shoes.

PROTECTION

Unlike roads, trails have rocks, sticks, brush, and pebbles that can poke and prod your feet. As a result, most trail shoes are built to be durable, with **beefier uppers** than road shoes. The **tightly woven mesh** of the upper keeps dirt from getting into your socks and irritating your feet. **Sturdier overlays** add structure to the upper for stability while also increasing a shoe's durability. **Heartier sidewalls** protect the sides of your feet from sticks and unexpected pokes. **Toe bumpers** save you from stubbing your toes. **Rock plates** keep pokey parts of the trail from jabbing the undersides of your feet. The **burlier outsoles** of trail shoes also provide protection underfoot.

[11] Midsole: Containing the shoe's cushioning, the midsole lies between your foot and the shoe's outsole. It is made of foam for softness and cushioning, and sometimes stability, and provides underfoot protection.

[12] Insole: A thin, usually removable, piece of foam inserted inside the shoe. Insoles vary in thickness and amount of arch support, and some have special antistink treatments.

[13] Cushioning: Soft foam in the midsole and padding around the heel collar and in the tongue. Amount of cushioning varies among shoes.

[14] **Medial post:** A firm piece of foam or rubber near the center of the medial side of trail shoe midsoles, meant to provide midfoot stability. Not found on all shoes.

[15] **Rock plate:** A thin, hard, yet flexible piece of material, usually made of plastic, sandwiched between the shoe's outsole and midsole. Intended to block sharp objects from jabbing soles. Not found on all shoes.

[16] **Offset:** The difference in height between the heel and the toe. Also called the "drop."

[17] **Outsole:** The underside of a shoe; the part that hits the ground. Made of some combination of varying types of rubber.

[18] **Flex grooves:** Cuts strategically placed in the outsole to allow the shoe to flex with your foot.

TIE ONE ON

Shoe tying runs the gamut from how you lace your shoes to what is used to tie them. Some laces stay tied better than others. Always double- or triple-knot your laces. If you have shoes with one-pull laces, be sure to tuck away the lace loop. Leaving it flopping can cause a nasty fall—tree branches snag loops, and excess laces cause tripping.

If you have lace-up shoes, you can use the eyelets to adjust a shoe's fit. The higher up the shoe you lace, the more secure the fit around the collar. You can also lessen pressure on various parts of your foot by lacing creatively.

[19] Lugs: Rubber protrusions located on the outsole and varying in size, shape, and quantity. Designed to provide better grip on trail surfaces.

Safety and performance features

Traction. Trails can be slippery due to steep inclines, loose dirt, slick mud, soft leaves, or wet roots and rocks. Even crushed-gravel paths have a lot more give than pavement does. Many trail shoes

YOU BIG LUG!

How much traction you need depends on the types of trails you'll be running and the conditions in which you'll be running them. Trail shoes grip the trail by using various kinds of traction. Lugs come in a variety of shapes and sizes—big, small, multidirectional, strategically spaced—and don't have to be hugely protruding to give you effective traction. Big lugs work in wet or loose dirt, but so do multidirectional lugs, strategically spaced out lugs, or aggressively shaped lugs. Some lugs protrude less than others, which is nice if some of your runs include paved sections. Sticky rubber on the bottom adds a Spider-Man effect, allowing you to grip rocky terrain, but does add some weight to a shoe.

If your run covers a combination of pavement and trail, look for a shoe with low-profile yet effective lugs (multidirectional, strategically spaced/placed). Large, protruding lugs or sticky rubber can make pavement sections feel laborious.

have an outsole built to give you stability and grip in challenging conditions. (See "Conditional Love," page 58.)

Flexibility. Trail shoes range in flexibility, from superbendy (it should flex where your forefoot naturally flexes) to stiff. How much you want your shoe to flex is a matter of personal preference. There are benefits to both types.

Flexible	vs.	Stiff
Nothing restricting your foot from flexing, especially uphill. Natural feel.		Protective underfoot. Can offer more support

Shopping-tip To test a shoe's flexibility, fold it in half (toe to heel) to see how easily it bends. Be sure to also put the shoe on and run around a little to make sure it flexes in places that are comfortable for your foot.

Weight. Trail shoes range in weight from barely there to beefy and heavy. Lighter-weight shoes sometimes offer less protection, but not always. And a heavy shoe is not automatically more protective; it may be heavy just because of the materials used. Make your selection based on fit, comfort, and the types of trails you will be running. The sweet spot is a well-balanced shoe that's lightweight enough *and* supportive/protective enough for your needs.

Fit. Fit is a key factor in deciding what trail shoe is right for you. Assess how it fits in length, width, and volume. A comfortable shoe equals a happy runner. (And, not surprisingly, the opposite is also often true.)

Offset. Shoes come in a range of "offsets," meaning the cushioning differential between the heel and the forefoot. Traditional shoes have around 12-mm offsets, whereas shoes aiming for a more natural ride come in offsets from 8 mm to zero. (*Note:* Our feet have zero offsets.)

SAYS WHO

"For the best control on the trail, look for a shoe that's secure in the heel and the midfoot so your foot doesn't slosh around. Make sure you have room at the end of your toes— around a thumbnail in length—and enough volume in the forefoot to allow room for your feet when running downhill and if/ when your feet swell."

HENRY GUZMAN, owner, Flatirons Running Inc., Boulder, Colorado

Getting All Dolled Up

TOPS

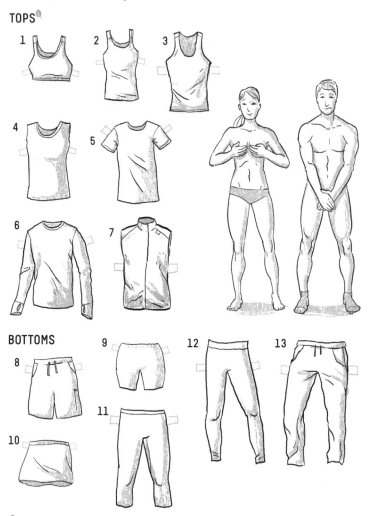

BOTTOMS

Jackets of all sorts are considered outerwear. For options, see page 47.

Apparel (aka "clothes")

You can run trails in your road running clothes. Heck, you can run trails in your boxer shorts or in no clothes at all (check local nudity ordinances). However, there are certain features to look for in apparel that can make you more comfortable on the trail.

Tops

[1] Sports bra. Offers great support and is more breathable, dries more quickly, and chafes less than a regular bra. There is no difference between a sports bra worn for trail running and one worn for road running or dodge ball. **BENEFITS:** Great support; can be worn beneath a shirt or by itself. **DOWNSIDE:** Can feel restrictive.

[2] Shimmel. A sports bra built like a tank top, covering the midsection. Some have pockets on the back to stash gels or keys. **BENEFITS:** Offers support but with more coverage than a sports bra. **DOWNSIDE:** Some shimmels are not as supportive as a sports bra.

[3] Singlet. Sleeveless top with narrow shoulder straps that allow maximum freedom of movement for swinging arms. Made of sweat-wicking, breathable, and lightweight technical fabric. Some have inset mesh panels to make them even cooler. **BENEFITS:** Cool; allows unrestricted arm swing; makes wearers look like serious runners. **DOWNSIDE:** Makes wearers look like serious runners.

[4] Tank top. Like a singlet but with wider shoulder straps. Made of sweat-wicking, breathable, lightweight technical fabric.

Some have mesh panels in high-sweat areas such as the center of the back. **BENEFITS:** Cool; a bit more sun protection and coverage than a singlet. **DOWNSIDE:** Gives you a teenage-lifeguard's tan.

[5] Short-sleeved shirt. Made of lightweight, breathable, and wicking material. Can be crew neck, V-neck, or zip neck; loose-fitting or tight; and may have mesh panels. **BENEFITS:** More sun protection and coverage than tanks; can be worn year-round (layered in winter). **DOWNSIDE:** Likelihood of a farmer's tan.

[6] Long-sleeved shirt. Made of technical fabrics to keep you comfortable when you sweat. Can be crew neck, V-neck, or zip neck. Some have thumbholes or fold-over cuffs to keep hands warm on cold days. **BENEFITS:** Can be worn alone or layered under a jacket; zippers can be undone for ventilation; ties easily around waist if you want to shed a layer. **DOWNSIDE:** Sleeves can be stifling if the weather gets hot.

[7] Vest. Can be made of lightweight, wind-shielding material with mesh on the back for ventilation or of fleece or softshell material meant to keep your core warm. **BENEFITS:** Keeps your core warm; can be worn over any type of shirt. **DOWNSIDE:** No sleeves to tie around your waist, making it tough to shed midrun.

Bottoms

[8] Shorts. Made of a lightweight, quick-drying exterior shell and a supportive (men) interior brief, running shorts come in a range of lengths, from short to long. Shorts with longer inseams provide more protection on the trail; plus, they look like casual

shorts, which is great if you head to the coffee shop postrun. Some have pockets to help runners stash keys,[Q] gels, or a phone. **BENEFITS:** Keep you cool; show off trail running legs. **DOWNSIDE:** Can cause midthigh chafing, depending on shorts style and body type.

[9] Boy shorts. Worn by women (as well as some male triathletes and German sunbathers), these small Lycra briefs fit snugly. **BENEFITS:** Eliminate chafing between thighs; offer some muscle support around hips and glutes; outline a nice rear end. **DOWNSIDE:** Not as cool as shorts because of the lack of airflow directly to the skin; outline any rear end.

[10] Skirt. Made from lightweight, quick-drying material. Skirts often have shorts underneath to keep things modest (or you can add your own), and those shorts often have pockets. **BENEFITS:** Covers your rear end; can eliminate chafing some-times caused by shorts; makes you feel girly in a dirt world. **DOWNSIDE:** Makes you feel girly in a dirt world.

[11] Capris. Usually tight-fitting and hitting somewhere between calf and knee. Ideal when it's too cold for shorts and too hot for tights or pants. Often have interior pockets and/or zippered back pockets. Popular choice for women, but some men wear them, too. Men in Capris instantly make themselves look European. **BENEFITS:** Eliminate chafing; offer some muscle support plus protection from brush; good length for

[Q] Consider **securing keys** in a zippered pocket when running trails, as getting stuck at a trailhead without the key that fell out halfway through a run makes for a long, logistically difficult day.

a range of weather conditions; outline a nice rear end. **DOWN-SIDE:** Can be too hot in summer; can leave you with cold ankles in winter; outline any rear end.

[12] Tights. Made from a range of materials, from superthin to thick and fleece-lined, some have an interior pocket and/or exterior zippered pocket in back. Tights snag less than pants do and minimize airflow between skin and fabric, which can make them warmer than pants. **BENEFITS:** Warm; fit close to the body to minimize snagging; offer some muscle support; can be layered under pants for added warmth. **DOWNSIDE:** Can be hot; don't leave much about a body to the imagination (especially when worn by men).

[13] Pants. Running pants offer a more casual look than tights do. They come in a range of weights and fabrics and usually have an internal key pocket as well as external pockets for carrying items and lending them their casual look. **BENEFITS:** Warmth and coverage in cold weather; easily layered over shorts or tights; can be worn to grocery store postrun. **DOWNSIDE:** Let air circulate between skin and fabric, which can feel cold on cold days; can snag on brush; can feel floppy while running if too baggy.

 THE DIRT Capri pants originated in Capri, Italy, which is why the word is often capitalized.

(DON'T BE) SHELL-SHOCKED

Running jackets are not all created equal. They come in a range of weights and functionality.

Water-resistant or waterproof

Water-resistant. (1) Keeps you dry in light rain or snow, briefly (likely long enough to run back to your car). (2) Often lighter than a waterproof version, making it easy to pull out in a surprise attack of inclement weather and then stow when the rain or snow passes.

vs.

Waterproof. (1) Keeps you dry in a deluge for long periods of time. (2) Some have hoods that can be folded down or removed so they don't flop around when not in use.

Hardshell, softshell, or windshell

Hardshell. Waterproof, sealing out any water. Many achieve breathability by having ventilation panels in high-sweat zones, such as underarms and midback. Most have hoods (some are removable). Hardshell jacket fabric tends to make a swish-swish noise when you swing your arms. Some have zip-off arms to become vests.

vs.

Softshell. Water-resistant/-repellent and allows air to pass through, making softshell fabric more breathable

---

To make running in them comfortable, waterproof jackets should have a **breathability** factor—whether the fabric itself has inherent breathability or the jacket has ventilation ports or panels built into it.

Continued

than hardshell fabric. Softshells also tend to be thicker than hardshells and can provide more warmth (unless a hardshell doesn't ventilate and causes uncomfortable overheating when running). Softshell material is generally quiet when you swing your arms.

vs.

Windshell. Made of a nonpermeable fabric such as nylon, windshells keep cold wind from chilling you and can ward off a light snow or wind. Windshells are not waterproof, so they become wet from precipitation and ample perspiration. Windshells are generally more lightweight than hardshells or softshells.

Some **windshells** are treated with a durable water repellency (DWR) coating to improve their ability to block and shed rain and snow.

 Shopping-tip Any jacket you wear running, aside from puffy or fleecy contraptions made for dead-of-winter outings, should be compressible enough to stuff in a pack and light enough to be tied around your waist. When shopping, try smashing the jacket down to a compact size, and also try tying it around your waist to see if it stays put.

No Hard-and-Fast Fashion Rules for Trail Running Wear

Defiant Mountain Runner Dude. Some trail runners have been known to run in jeans and a flannel shirt, carrying nothing more than a plastic soda bottle.

Speed Racer. Some run in precariously small shorts, minimal shoes, and no socks. Pace-tracking device is the only thing causing drag.

Ultrarunning Hipster. Trail running hipsters can often be found in thick-rimmed, Ray-Ban-style sunglasses and trucker hats. Some run while chatting on cell phones, texting, and Tweeting.

THE BOTTOM LINE There are no fashion rules in trail running; you can run in whatever you want. Feel free to express your individuality—but remember, the goal is to be as comfortable as possible, and it doesn't hurt to choose apparel that prepares you for whatever the trail throws your way.

Accessories

The right-sized hydration system, lightweight sunglasses, and a visor can tie your trail running outfit together better than a bracelet to a dress or a manpurse to a suit.

Accessorize your trail running with items that help you stay out longer and enjoy your run more.

Fluid-carrying devices

Known as "hydration systems," these contraptions are made to carry fluids while running. They come in various forms, and there are pros and cons to using each type.

Handheld

PROS	CONS
Comes in small volume.	Can cause muscle imbalances if carrying in only one hand.
Ease of use encourages frequent drinking.	Tricky if you need your hands to maneuver complicated trails.
Easy to refill at aid stations during races.	

 Switch hands often.

 Handhelds come with an adjustable carrying strap. This frees your hand for tasks such as tying shoes and climbing steep, rocky sections hand-over-foot and also gives your hand muscles a break.

Waist belt with one or more bottles

PROS	CONS
Frees your hands.	Can be bouncy.
Distributes weight at your center of gravity.	Tricky to access if bottles are in the back.
Usually has pockets for phone, gels, or keys.	
Can fill bottles with different fluids: one with water, one with sports drink, etc.	Can feel restricting around the waist.

Backpack

PROS	CONS
Frees hands.	Can feel hot on a warm day
For packs with a bladder, the hydration hose up front ensures easy drinking.	Can feel constricting.
Models with bottles usually distribute bottle weight evenly via pockets on back and/or chest.	Bladder is less accessible, so can be a pain to refill midrun (e.g., during a long race).
Able to carry phone, gels, jacket, and other needs. Allows for self-sufficiency and longer outings.	

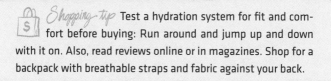 *Shopping tip* Test a hydration system for fit and comfort before buying: Run around and jump up and down with it on. Also, read reviews online or in magazines. Shop for a backpack with breathable straps and fabric against your back.

 Experiment with different **placements of the belt** to increase comfort. For example, wear it around your hip bones instead of around your waist.

 Backpacks should have straps that adjust to how tightly you want the pack secured and where you want it to rest on your body. Play with the adjustments to make them as comfortable as possible for your body type.

Socks

One of the delights of trail running is getting close to nature. And sometimes nature wants to get really close to you, too—like right into your socks. Trails are rich with dirt, pebbles, sticks, or brush that can irritate your feet and cause blisters and other discomfort. (See "Blisters," page 136.) For that reason, it's best to wear socks that extend at least over your anklebone, erecting a barrier between nature and your skin. When temperatures drop, wear socks that bridge the gap between your shoes and your tights or running pants. Exposed skin at the ankles can be uncomfortable.

Headwear

Not to be confused with headgear, headwear for trail running has myriad uses, from sun-shielding to warmth-maintaining to sweat-controlling. (None of these will help with your overbite, however.)

- Baseball-style running **caps** offer a sun-shielding bill and should be breathable, lightweight, and quick-drying. Official Red Sox (or Yankees) caps work, too . . . they're just hotter and take longer to dry. Trucker hats with their plastic mesh and oversized front panels have the added bonus of making you appear hiply retro.

- Topless **hats** (called visors) provide sun protection and shade and wick sweat from your brow. A cooler choice on hot days.

- Made of lightweight wool, fleece, or other wicking synthetic material, **beanies** provide warmth. While you can wear a thick, fuzzy ski hat with a poofy ball on top, a thin beanie is easier to stuff into your backpack or a pocket if you get hot midrun.

- Made of terrycloth or other stretchy, sweat-wicking material, **headbands** can be worn several ways. Worn across your brow, they keep perspiration from running into your eyes and make you look like Roger Federer or an NBA player. Worn farther back, they keep your hair at bay while making you look like a yoga instructor or female soccer player. Worn over hair to hold it down, they give you the appearance of a 20-year-old male soccer player or a flower child.

Sunglasses

Running sunglasses should be lightweight and fog-resistant and should stay put despite sweat (grippy nose bridges and temples help). Styles range from wide-coverage, one-piece lenses that act as eye shields to hip-looking, casual shades. Lenses vary from light to dark, polarized (extra protective) to UV-blocking (at the very least) to lenses that change shade based on light conditions. Some sunglasses come with lenses that can be swapped out based on the conditions.

Shopping tip When trying on sunglasses, ensure that they stay put when propped on your head. Since trails dip in and out of tree cover, you may want to remove your glasses at times during a run.

Wrist computers

The most basic computerized wrist device is known as a **watch**. A simple watch that tells time and has, perhaps, a chronograph (aka: stopwatch) is sufficient for a trail run. (If you don't have to be anywhere or know how long a run usually takes, not wearing a watch works well, too.)

Fancy features:

- **GPS-enabled gadgets** track your time and distance, map your route, and allow you to upload your data to your computer and the Internet and to obsess over compare it with other runners, or with your own runs on other days.

- An **altimeter** tells you your current elevation plus overall accumulated gain and loss. Helpful for navigation purposes, and for obsessing over training.

- A **barometer** measures barometric pressure and gives you clues as to what weather to expect on a run. Useful to runners planning long or multiday runs or who don't trust weather reporters.

- **Heart rate monitors** gauge your effort while running. You can even program them to beep at you if you're running too slow or too hard. Good for obsessing over training and useful for pacing yourself during a tempo run or race.

Arm warmers/coolers

Made of thin, lightweight, wicking fabric—synthetic, wool, or a combination of the two—arm warmers keep your arms warm. They are easy to take off and stow when the temperature rises.

Arm coolers look the same as arm warmers but are made of technical fabrics meant to make your skin cooler when wet and also offer some protection from the sun. Arm coolers are often white.

Compression gear

Socks and calf sleeves, as well as tights and shorts that fit snugly and have strategically placed compressive paneling, are called "compression gear." These items are said to increase circulation, support muscles, and improve recovery. Some trail runners swear by them (especially long compression socks because, among other things, they help protect lower legs from brush).

Gaiters

Gaiters keep debris or snow from sneaking into shoes and socks. They attach to the top of the shoe, are generally short, and are made of stretchy, breathable material. Gaiters are often worn by runners expecting messy conditions, such as tall brush, deep sand, fields of shale, or snow.

Compression socks are also a warming choice when it's too cool for shorts but not cold enough for tights or pants. Or they can be worn underneath pants or tights for an added layer of warmth.

Trekking poles

Popular in Europe, trekking poles are handy tools for runners when large and/or multiple mountains are being climbed and descended. Having one or two in hand takes pressure off your feet and legs and helps stabilize you on the trail. Ideally, poles used for trail running collapse down to the size of a wizard's wand and can be stashed in or attached to a runner's backpack or carried in one hand when not in use.

Filtration systems

Runners who spend long periods of time on remote runs often carry a filtration system, allowing them to take water from streams, rivers, or lakes. Filtration systems range from iodine drops or tinctures (small and lightweight; work in roughly 30 minutes; make water taste funny) to mechanical filters (such as a water-sterilizing, penlike contraption that filters water quickly and easily). All can be found at outdoor stores or online. (See "Filtering/ Treating Water," page 90, for filtration options.)

First aid lite

On short trail runs in mild conditions, you can probably get away with not bringing any first-aid supplies on your run. However, to be better safe than sorry, consider carrying one or all of the following, some of which come in easily packed single-use packets. (For more detail on first aid, see Chapter 8.)

What	Why?
Cell phone	To call for help
Ibuprofen/anti-inflammatory	To cut down swelling and pain
Band-Aid	To cover blisters or cuts
Topical antibiotic	To clean wounds
Antihistamine	To calm allergic reactions to bee stings, pollen, etc.

CHAPTER 5

How: Conditions

While you can head out on a trail run without much thought or strategy, wise choices about gear, where to go, and how to handle yourself can make your experiences more enjoyable—even the ones that sometimes kind of aren't. (It's okay to have a bad run once in a while.) Tough runs in challenging conditions happen. But don't let unpreparedness or unwillingness to embrace adversity be the problem.

Being a trail runner means being adaptable—a great skill to master in running and in life. Know-how makes being adaptable a lot easier and can keep you sure-footed and confident on everything from an icy trail to a first date.

Conditional love

Whether you're facing a foot of snow on the ground or dealing with wildly encroaching grasses, smart tactical decisions allow you to embrace trail conditions of all sorts.

Ice

Ice-coated trails and tree branches can turn your world into a breathtaking winter wonderland, making you forget about dangers underfoot. Don't. Be mindful of not only visible ice but also icy trails buried beneath fresh snow and "black ice" (also known as "clear ice"), a thin layer of ice glazed over rocks, dirt, or pavement.

Wear this. Traction is key. Several options for adding traction exist, from lightweight, slip-on traction devices to installing screws into your shoe sole to shoes that come equipped with built-in retractable carbide spikes. ≋ Gloves protect your hands if you do slip and fall.

> *Shopping tip* Slip-on traction devices slide over your shoes. Since you may take them off and put them back on a few times during a run, shop for a pair that can be stashed in your hydration pack, stuffed in the back waistband of your tights or pants, or carried comfortably in hand.

Do this. Choose trails wisely—trails facing north don't get as much sun as do trails facing south (the opposite holds true in the Southern Hemisphere), so they can be icier. ≋ Trails protected by tree cover will be icier than will trails in open fields and meadows. ≋ Seek out crunchy, broken snow (sometimes found on the sides of trails) instead of smooth snow, which can be hard-packed and icy. ≋ Trails are most slick in the late afternoon and early evening after a warm day may have melted some snow and it begins to refreeze. Plan accordingly.

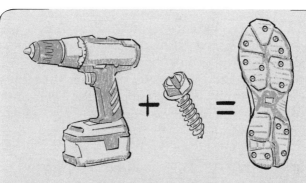

DIY: SCREW SHOES

1. Buy 20 to 40 number-8 ⅜-inch or ½-inch-long sheet-metal screws from the hardware store. (They should cost you no more than $4.)

2. Find a drill with a magnetic tip.

3. Choose a pair of shoes that are good for wintry conditions (i.e., don't reach for your most breathable pair).

4. Mark the bottoms of the shoes with an X in the spots where you want toothy, ice-gripping traction.

5. Use a drill bit to drill holes on your Xs.

6. Use the magnetic drill tip with ¼-inch socket attachment to insert one screw at a time into the holes on your Xs.

If your shoes are particularly **thin-soled**, opt for number-6 ¼-inch screws.

Follow the **tread patterns** existing on the shoe—make your Xs on the most protruding part of the existing traction. Make 8 to 12 Xs on the forefoot and 4 to 8 Xs on the rearfoot.

At the end of icy season, use the reverse-direction setting on your drill to **remove the screws**. There will be minimal holes barely visible in the sole, and the shoes will be fine.

Snow

Fresh snow or falling snow mutes sound and creates the quietest trail you may ever experience. It also makes for cold ankles if you don't dress appropriately and works your core as you stabilize (see "Home Improvement," page 202, for core-strengthening exercises). If you run in deep snow without the proper gear (i.e., snowshoes), be ready for some postholing.

Postholing \pōst-hōl-ing\ v. 1. Taking a step on what you hope is firm snow, only to find your foot sinking in as deep as your thigh. 2. A (very) challenging way to get through a trail run.

Wear this. If the trail is covered in only a few inches of fresh snow, there may be no need for special footwear. If new snow is on top of old snow, however, traction is recommended, as the old snow underneath can be icy. 🌊 If the snow is deep, snowshoes meant for running are recommended. 🌊 Bundle up, but wisely. Long pants or tights and socks (wool socks provide breathable warmth and moisture management) that bridge the gap between your shoes and bottoms will keep you warm. Layer on your top half, and wear gloves and a breathable beanie.

Do this. Seek out crunchy, broken snow (sometimes found on the sides of trails), which is less slippery than smooth snow. 🌊 Trails are most slick in the late afternoon and early evening after a warm day might have melted some snow and it begins to refreeze. Plan accordingly.

Shoes made of waterproof materials keep feet dry, but some don't breathe well and keep sweaty feet wet. These materials can also make a shoe stiff and heavy. Consider wearing regular trail running shoes with thick wool socks.

SNOWSHOE RUNNING: IT'S EASIER THAN YOU THINK

Snowshoe running can take place anywhere there is enough snow: a snow-covered trail, fire road, quiet neighborhood road, Nordic center with snowshoe trails, or anywhere in the woods (snow cover makes trails unnecessary).

Trails used for snowmobiling make great snowshoe trails because they're wide and packed down. (Just keep an ear out for snowmobiles, and move to the side when they're coming.)

Wear snowshoes made for running, and run as you would ordinarily but with a slightly wider stance in order to avoid kicking your anklebone with the snowshoe frame on the opposite foot. On downhills, let your landing foot glide in the snow for a split second before picking it up for your next step.

Don't run on tracked Nordic trails (the holes punched by your snowshoes mess up the skiable terrain) or on snowmobile trails that don't allow foot traffic. Research snowmobile trails in your area for restrictions and information.

Snowshoe running is a great workout that burns more calories per hour than regular running and really works your glutes, quads, and hip flexors. And if you want to test your mettle, snowshoe races—usually 5K or 10K—are a fun way to spice up your winter running.

WHAT TO WEAR

- **Snowshoes made for running.** Running snowshoes are smaller and lighter than regular snowshoes and often have tapered frames for a less-encumbered stride.
- **Running shoes.** Consider waterproof shoes if they're light and flexible; if not, wear regular trail or road shoes with thick socks or waterproof/neoprene socks. Traction comes from the snowshoe, so it's not important to wear a shoe with good traction.
- **Tall, thick socks.** It's important to keep feet, ankles, and lower legs warm. If the snow is deep, if it's very cold, or if you'll be forging a trail in deep snow, wear waterproof socks to help keep feet dry.
- **Gaiters.** These keep snow from getting inside shoes.
- **Bottom half.** Tights with a smooth exterior work best, as snow clings to fleecy exteriors when kicked up from your snowshoes. Pants can be colder due to the looser fit, and a loose opening at the ankle potentially allows snow to sneak in.
- **Top half.** Layer, because you'll get hot. A long-sleeved technical shirt and breathable jacket work for most winter conditions. Very cold temperatures may require

a second shirt, a midlayer, and/or a thicker jacket.

- **Beanie.** A beanie keeps your head warm. If you need to shed it once you've warmed up, you can tuck it into your waistband.
- **Cap.** A billed cap keeps falling snow off your face. If it's cold, add a thin beanie underneath.
- **Gloves.** Wear thin to medium-thin gloves to keep your hands warm, protect them should you fall, and help you comfortably grab an aspen tree or two along the trail to help get up a hill. Store in your waistband if you begin to overheat.
- **Sunglasses.** These shield eyes from snow and sun; sun reflects off snow, making it twice as bright.
- **Poles.** These are needed only if a steep uphill requires hiking for long periods.

Overgrown trail

Sometimes tall grasses, bushes, or whatever grows along the sides of the trail overtake your path. This can make for a fun junglelike adventure. But since you don't want to carry a machete, know that bare legs will likely get itchy and scratchy, and you might get burrs or prickers in your socks. You may wade through rash-inducing—or bug-rich—flora. And not being able to see the trail underfoot can create ankle-twisting hazards.

Wear this. Tall socks, pants or tights, and a long-sleeved shirt or arm warmers/coolers keep skin from getting scratched. ⟱ Consider bug spray.

Do this. Find another route, and wait until fall or winter to return to this trail. Late spring and summer usually bring the most overgrown conditions. ≋ Forge ahead, paying attention to footing by taking shorter strides and placing your feet flat with every step. ≋ Check your body for ticks and/or chiggers after your run, depending on where you ran. ≋ If running with others, take care to not whack those behind you with a branch you push aside. ≋ Consider volunteering with a trail maintenance group.

Poisonous plants

Poison ivy, poison oak, and sumac plants are more prevalent in some regions and seasons; for instance, coastal California in the springtime is rife with poison oak. Poison ivy grows in places such as Virginia's Shenandoah National Park. Sumac grows mostly in the Southeast and Midwest. All three have urushiol oils that can irritate the skin.

Wear this. Cover as much of your body as possible without making you overheat: long pants or tights; Capris or shorts with long socks; lightweight, breathable long-sleeved shirt; short-sleeved shirt with arm warmers/coolers.

Do this. If you know you're allergic, search online for "poison oak/ poison ivy/poison sumac in [place where you plan to run]." ≋ Know what the plants look like. Remember: *Leaves of three, let it be.* (See "Plant-Inflicted Hazards," page 146.) ≋ If you encounter poisonous plants, as soon as possible, thoroughly rub down any

---

Not everyone is allergic to the oil—called **urushiol** ("you-ROO-shee-all")—found on poison ivy, oak, and sumac. If you've never had a rash from contact with one of these plants but live and run in areas where they grow, you may be one of the lucky 15 percent of resistant Americans.

exposed skin with rubbing alcohol or with a poison oak and ivy oil removal solution, available over the counter at most pharmacies. ⛆ Rinse for longer than you think you need to. (See "How to: Lessen or Avoid a Rash from Toxic Plant Oils," page 147.)

> ☀ If you know you will be running in an area where you're
> TIP likely to be exposed, keep oil-removal soap or rubbing
> alcohol wipes in your car or in your running pack and scrub down
> as soon as possible. The sooner you remove the oil, the less
> likely it is to spread.

Sand

If you're running on a beach or in a desert, prepare for a great strength workout. Enjoy the beauty, but be aware that tiny sand granules will do their best to creep into your shoes and socks and irritate your feet.

Wear this. Shoes with closed mesh. ⛆ In extreme situations (like, if you're racing across the Sahara Desert for days on end), wear gaiters and waterproof/neoprene socks to keep sand from irritating your feet. (See "Blisters," page 136.)

Do this. Embrace the strength training! ⛆ If you're near a body of water, running close to the water's edge will likely give you harder-packed sand for an easier running surface. ⛆ If you're in a desert, descend sand dunes by gliding on your landing foot for a second before taking another step. ⛆ Keep your core engaged and drive your arms for additional power.

Mud

A few rainy days or melting snow can turn your favorite trail into a slippery, sloppy mud pit. Remember how it felt to be a kid playing in the mud? Revel in getting dirty, and know that running in slippery goop will tax your body similarly to running in sand and snow—you'll be using your core for stability.

Wear this. Quick-drying socks. ≋ Shoes that drain water well with rugged traction patterns on the soles. ≋ Capris, tights, or shorts—nothing baggy around your legs and ankles that could become bogged down with mud.

Do this. To best preserve trails, stay off them when they're muddy. ≋ If you find yourself on a muddy trail, run down the middle. Skirting around the mud widens the trail and damages the area that surrounds it. ≋ Seek out trails on south-facing slopes or in treeless areas—the more a trail is exposed to the sun, the drier it should be. ≋ Run early in the day, when the ground is likely colder. Warmth later in the day can turn a frozen trail into a muddy one. ≋ Know the types of dirt on the trails you run. Sandy soils fare better in moisture than do clay. Wet clay soil clings to shoes in clumps, making them ridiculously heavy.

> TIP To clean muddy shoes, spray them with a hose and let them dry in the sun. Stuffing newspaper inside them will quicken drying times. Alternately, wait until the mud dries, then bang shoes together vigorously—watching out for flying mud.

Dark

Running at night or in the predawn may be your only option on a busy day, especially during the short days of winter. Running in the dark can make you feel like a rebel. While everyone else is in their homes, cozy and sheltered, you're out on the trail with the other nocturnal animals. (See Chapter 7 for the scoop on creatures to be aware of.)

Wear this. A headlamp or flashlight. Something reflective if your run includes portions of pavement/street.

Headlamp and flashlight **brightness** is measured by lumens. The higher the lumen count, the brighter the light. Other factors in light effectiveness are the width and angle of the beam, how many feet ahead it illuminates, and how long it burns before you have to change batteries.

Some backpacks and waistpacks have **lights** mounted at chest and waist level, which leave hands free and illuminate from a point closer to the ground.

Do this. Go with a buddy, either human or animal. There's safety in numbers. ≋ Make noise—talk, sing, cackle—so animals know you're human and not deer meat.

Weather the weather

Neither snow nor rain nor heat nor gloom of night need keep a trail runner indoors. Smart gear choices, a little knowledge, and a taste for adventure enable you to get outside in adverse elements.

Heat

High temperatures and a scorching sun up the risk of dehydration and sunburn. But these conditions don't have to be uncomfortable.

Wear this. Minimal clothing or lightweight short- or long-sleeved shirts that are very breathable (such as mesh), are quick-drying, and possibly have cooling yarns built into the fabrics. ≋ Sun-blocking hat or visor. ≋ Sunblock. ≋ Hydration system filled with electrolytes mixed with water. (See Chapter 6 for more on hydration.)

Do this. Run early or late rather than at midday. ≋ Choose trails with tree cover. ≋ Bring plenty of liquids with electrolytes. ≋ Add ice to your liquids to keep them cold. ≋ Squirt water on the back of your neck or head.

The back of the neck or the temples, just in front of your ears, are the most effective **cooling spots**. Squirt water on those spots to stay cool.

Humidity

Yes, humidity can make you feel like you're trying to breathe underwater. And humidity makes you incredibly sweaty because your sweat doesn't evaporate off your body. But, heck, a lot of people sit in saunas on purpose, right? Embrace it!

Wear this. Mesh or other superlight, superbreathable fabrics that allow skin to sweat and then wick sweat away. ≡ Shorts/skirts made from lightweight, breathable, quick-drying materials. (Don't wear anything that will make you feel more bogged down than the humidity does already.) ≡ A hat, visor, or headband with wicking material at the brow to help keep sweat out of your eyes. ≡ Hydration system (see "Fluid-Carrying Devices," page 50) with electrolyte replacement fluids (see "Hydration," page 96).

Do this. Bring extra fluids with electrolyte replacement. ≡ Add ice cubes to fluids. ≡ Occasionally squirt the back of your neck or temples to help you stay cool and refreshed. ≡ Run after a rainstorm, as the humidity is often lower once the clouds clear.

Cold

It can be hard to feel motivated when it's cold outside. Remind yourself that the coldest you are likely to be is the few seconds between stepping out the door and starting your run. Plus, it's fun to see your breath, isn't it?

 Our breath contains **water vapor**. Cold air makes it condense into a fog.

Wear this. Tights are generally warmer than pants, as tights hug your skin while pants let air circulate between skin and fabric. ≋ Snug-fitting, long-sleeved shirt, possibly a midlayer or second shirt, and/or a running jacket. ≋ Gloves/mittens. ≋ Beanie that covers ears or ear warmers. ⚐ ≋ Long, warm socks that close gaps between socks and tights. ≋ A face gaiter. ≋ Sunglasses to keep eyes from tearing up in cold.

Do this. Shorten your run if necessary, knowing your body burns energy simply trying to stay warm. ≋ Run midday, or check hourly weather reports for the warmest time of the day (taking note of wind-chill factors).

Dryness

Dry climates remain dry through hot and cold temperatures. A lack of moisture in the air exists at high altitude and in desert environments, and while you may appreciate the feeling of less sweat due to evaporation, dryness increases thirst.

Wear this. A hydration system loaded with electrolyte replacement. ≋ Lip balm. ≋ Sunblock or other lotion to protect skin.

Do this. Drink often, even if you feel like you're not sweating—it's just evaporating quickly.

 Mittens are generally warmer than gloves due to your fingers' ability to provide body heat to each other.
   Ball up cold fingers in your gloves or mittens to benefit from the body heat generated by your palms and fingers together.

 Don't wear **earrings** on cold runs. The metal draws cold to your ears.

Wind

Wind can be a drag, literally, creating unwelcome resistance training. But look at the bright side: Resistance training makes you
stronger, and wind that blows around leaves and trees is a lot more
interesting than the wind that comes out of a fan at the gym.

Wear this. Windshell (if the temperature is cool). Sunglasses
(try light or clear lenses if running in low light) to shield eyes from
wind and any flying debris.

Do this. Choose a trail sheltered by thick trees or with a hillside
to block the wind. Wind whipping in from the west? Run on a
trail on the eastern flank of a hill. Check the weather reports
for wind forecasts, and aim to run when the wind is predicted at
lower speeds.

 Leave **hats** with bills or visors at home on a windy day—they are likely to blow off.

Rain

Running in the rain can be great fun. Sure, rain can make trails messy. And being wet increases the potential for chafing. But think how much fun kids (and dogs and birds, and soon . . . you) have splashing in puddles.

Wear this. Billed cap to keep rain off your face. ≋ Breathable waterproof or water-resistant jacket. ≋ Thin, quick-drying clothing that fits closely (to avoid it sloshing about when wet). ≋ Shoes that drain water well and have good traction.

Do this. Seek out a trail with overhead tree protection—this will help keep you and the trail dry. ≋ Seek out a trail made of crushed gravel or firm dirt or covered in leaves. Dusty, soft-dirt trails turn quickly to slippery mud in rainy conditions.

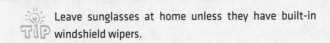

Leave sunglasses at home unless they have built-in windshield wipers.

Snow

Running in everything from a lightly falling snow to a full-on winter dumping can make you feel like a Siberian tiger—free to roam and fearful of nothing. So while it is true that footing can become increasingly challenging as the snow falls, and sideways snow can pelt your face, embrace it and run on!

Wear this. Billed hat to block snow from your face. ≋ Tights or pants with narrow ankle cuffs to help keep snow from creeping in. ≋ Long socks to keep you warm and protect skin from snow. ≋ Thin, long-sleeved shirt, potentially a second long-sleeved shirt or midlayer, and/or a jacket that sheds snow (a soft-shell jacket is ideal). ≋ Shoes with good traction or with traction devices or screws (see "Ice," page 60.) ≋ Gloves or mittens.

Do this. If snow is blowing sideways or it's snowing a lot, seek out a trail with protection from dense, large trees. ≋ Seek out crunchy snow. It's less slippery than smooth snow. ≋ Run in the morning when snow is fresh or at midday, when frozen snow has had a chance to warm and soften up. Try to avoid evenings, when melted snow may have iced up again, depending on temperatures.

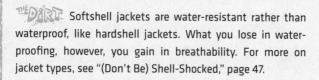 Softshell jackets are water-resistant rather than waterproof, like hardshell jackets. What you lose in water-proofing, however, you gain in breathability. For more on jacket types, see "(Don't Be) Shell-Shocked," page 47.

Whereabouts

Certain environments—as remote as a Costa Rican jungle or as near as an urban one—call for more planning than do others.

Mountains

Running in mountains amid scenic peaks, babbling brooks, and wildflowers is a trail runner's delight. But weather can change quickly in the mountains, posing some challenges worth preparing for in advance. Getting caught in a thunderstorm at high altitude or in fast-dropping temperatures can dampen an outing. And then there is the hilly terrain and possibly thin air.

Wear this. Sunglasses to protect eyes from strong sun at high elevations. ≋ Sunblock to protect skin at high elevations. ≋ Beanie for changing weather. ≋ Lightweight gloves for warmth in changing weather. ≋ Lightweight, water-resistant or waterproof shell for changing weather. ≋ A pack with enough capacity to carry the shell when not in use (or tie shell around your waist).

Do this. Carry sufficient fluids and energy to stay well hydrated and fed at high altitude. ≋ Make sure pack or pockets have capacity for a shell, beanie, and gloves. ≋ Check weather reports for thunderstorms or other weather hazards. ≋ Know that responsible mountaineers turn around by noon, whether they've reached the peaks or passes they're climbing toward or not. Follow suit.

Beach

Running on a beach can be hard work, but like all hard work, it has its rewards. It's beautiful, for one. And the sound of waves crashing and water lapping at your feet? The stuff of poetry.

Wear this. Shoes with tight mesh to minimize sand in your shoes. ≋ Thin, lightweight, quick-drying socks in case your feet get wet. ≋ A bathing suit under your running clothes, if desired. (Men, think more triathlon/swimsuit than board shorts.)

Do this. Check local tide charts and aim to run at low tide—that's when you'll have more hard-packed sand versus soft and are less apt to be halted by waves crashing against sea walls and other borders. ≋ Splash water on your face and neck after a hot run—or, heck, kick off your shoes and socks and just jump right in.

 THE DIRT Hard-packed sand near the shoreline is easier to run on than deep sand.

Jungle/Rainforest

If you run in a jungle or rainforest environment, prepare for heat, humidity, sudden rainstorms, and the possibility of leeches, wild boar, and snakes. The biggest danger, however, is likely to be your feet becoming wet and soggy (see "Blisters," page 136, for blister prevention and treatment).

Wear this. Shoes with good traction that drain water and dry quickly. ≋ Lightweight, wicking, quick-drying clothing. ≋ Hat or visor with built-in sweat-wicking headband. ≋ Hydration system to stay hydrated in intense heat and humidity. ≋ If bushwhacking is required, wear long, lightweight pants or tights and a long, lightweight shirt to cover up exposed skin to ward off leech-sucking.

Do this. Know where you're going. ≋ Be ready for slick surfaces. There's a reason they're called "rainforests." (See "Mud," page 68.)

bushwhacking \boosh-hwak-ing\ *v.* 1. Traveling off trail, through anything from malleable prairie grass to skin-cutting manzanita to beastly jungle vines. 2. A practice that should be minimized by recreationalists in an effort to preserve the environment. 3. A practice sometimes unavoidable by recreationalists who get lost, compete in adventure races, or step off trail to relieve themselves.

Urban jungle

Trail runners in urban jungles sometimes find themselves negotiating pavement, car traffic, crowds, and noises of the unnatural sort. These require careful maneuvering. Exposure to society can be shocking for both parties.

Wear this. Clothing you'd feel comfortable wearing walking into a 7-Eleven to buy a soda or to take a bus home post–trail run. Shoes that run comfortably on trails and pavement alike if your urban trail runs include road sections.

Do this. Carry a small amount of money with you for a snack/drink or in case you want to take a bus or cab home. Run headphone-free. Urban jungles are filled with hazards—if you can hear said hazards, you can better avoid them.

Navigating social situations

Follow these guidelines for social survival.

Postrun errands/kaffeeklatsches/pub-hopping

If you feel self-conscious about your tights hugging your buns in the checkout line at the market or baring too much leg while on a barstool, plan ahead. Also, expect to be dirty or sweaty enough that people around you notice. If that bothers you, plan accordingly.

kaffeeklatsch \ka-fey-klatsh\ *n.* 1. A German word meaning "getting together for coffee and conversation." 2. A casual environment for a postrun date.

Wear this. Running pants instead of tights, shorts over tights, a running skirt over Capris, or long shorts. 🥤 Quick-drying apparel that wards off stink (either naturally, like wool, or with an antimicrobial treatment).

Do this. Bring regular clothes for a quick change in your car. 🥤 Store body-cleansing wipes in your car for a postrun wipe-down. 🥤 Bring a sweatshirt or jacket to put on after your run, as you'll likely get cold as your sweat dries. 🥤 Bring a hat to cover up wild postrun hair.

Workday trail break

Turning your feet over on dirt amid nature can be just the reinvigoration you need to have a productive second half of your workday.

Logistics can be tricky, but the payoff is well worth it. Just be sure you don't lose yourself (by losing track of time or actually getting lost) on the trail.

Wear this. A watch.

Do this. Opt for a familiar run that you know will take you a set amount of time. ☰ Wear some of your running gear under/as your work clothes if possible to save time. ☰ Eat at your desk to allow more time for running. ☰ Invite your boss. This makes for great bonding time and eliminates the worry of getting busted for taking a long lunch.

Trail run date

A trail run can be the perfect date. There's no concern about who's buying, one party can always fake an injury and head back if the chemistry isn't great, or . . . singing birds and the beauty of the natural world can help foster a wonderful new romance. Be aware, however, that you may be thoroughly checked out during the run, and clingy running clothing can make this pretty easy to do.

Wear this. Trail running clothes you feel comfortable in from all angles—for instance, when running uphill in front of someone. ☰ An extra gel to offer if your date runs out or a bag of sports beans or chews you can share. ☰ Credit card or money for kaffee-klatsch or microbrew afterward.

Do this. Choose a scenic trail for the ambience. ☰ Be yourself. ☰ Fall in love—or don't.

CHAPTER 6

How: Nutrition

Gassing Up:
An Illustrated Metaphor

As a runner (and a human), food and drink are the fuel that makes you go. Good input means good output, and smart eating and drinking make a huge difference in how you feel on the run and in your everyday life.

Ready, set . . . vroom!

Preloading

What you eat and drink before setting out on a run is a highly personal matter. Some people need to eat a calculated meal exactly 2 hours and 17 minutes before they run. Others can inhale French toast or egg sandwiches on the way to the trailhead. And others don't eat a thing before heading out.

In order to operate properly during the run, preloading in the form of food and liquid is advised. Eating a mix of 80 percent carbohydrates and 20 percent protein two or three hours before a run is recommended. However, planning so far in advance is often unrealistic, especially if you're an early-morning runner. Trial and error will teach you whether you can inhale a bagel with peanut butter 20 minutes before heading out the door without feeling like you might barf.

> **TIP** If eating before a morning run simply won't work for you, eat a hearty dinner the night before, and maybe a late-night snack, and hydrate properly. That way you can skip eating before your run (but you should carry fluids and fuel with you, depending on the length of time you'll be out).

The better fueled and hydrated you are before the run, the less your body needs during the run—and the less you'll have to carry with you to maintain energy. Fill your tank before your run, and run on the gas in the tank, topping off when necessary.

On the run

Eating and drinking while running can be tricky. Figuring how much you need under what circumstances and what to carry and ingest takes some thought and planning.

How much do you need to eat and drink on the trail?

Though everyone is different and runs vary, generally speaking runners burn (and therefore need) roughly 4 carbohydrate calories per minute, or 240 calories per hour. That means that most of us cannot digest more than 240 calories an hour, no matter how much we eat. This is important to know because when food sits in your stomach undigested, gastrointestinal distress can ensue. On the flip side, if you don't ingest enough calories during your run, bonking is likely (see "Bonk," page 89). Ergo, figuring out what you need is important.

SOME FACTORS THAT AFFECT HOW MUCH YOU NEED TO FUEL AND HYDRATE

Factor	Answer	Need
How much do you weigh?	A lot	⬆ 💧 🍌
	A little	⬇ 💧 🍌
Are you male or female?	Male	⬆ 💧 🍌
	Female	⬇ 💧 🍌
How much did you eat before your run?	A lot	⬇ 🍌
	A little	⬆ 🍌
How much did you drink before your run?	A lot	⬇ 💧
	A little	⬆ 💧
Did you consume alcohol the night before your run?	Yes	⬆ 💧
	No	⬇ 💧
What's the temperature?	Hot	⬆ 💧
	Cold	⬆ 🍌
How long will you run?	Long	⬆ 💧 🍌
	Short	⬇ 💧 🍌
What kind of workout did you do yesterday?	Hard	⬆ 💧 🍌
	Easy/off	⬇ 💧 🍌
What kind of workout will you do tomorrow?	Hard	⬆ 💧 🍌
	Easy /off	⬇ 💧 🍌

While **beer and wine** can actually be good for you (see "Care and Feeding of a Trail Runner," page 100), minimizing alcohol intake the night before a big run or race can help mitigate dehydration the next day.

A runner's fluid and fuel needs on the run depend on several factors. Gender, weight, and prerun hydration and fueling all matter. Too, how much sweat you lose during a run should be factored into how much to drink while running. Sweat rates vary between .5 liter and 3 liters per hour and are not dependent on gender or size. To gauge how much you need to replenish, calculate your personal sweat rate. (See "Measuring Your Sweat Rate," page 88.)

The best way to figure out what you need is through trial and error, paying close attention to how you feel and listening to the messages your body is sending. A lot depends on how far you're running, the temperature, and other factors.

Bathroom monitor

What do smart hydration and fueling have to do with a toilet and a scale? Turns out, a lot. Both are very useful tools for assessing how well you are hydrating and for knowing how quickly your body digests food.

Corn test. Knowing how quickly your body processes what you eat will help you figure what you'll need on the run. Try the corn test: Eat corn at dinner one night, and see how long it takes to, um . . . show up. Happen quickly? You may need more food on the run than you think. Happen slowly? You may need less food on the run than you think. (And if fueling up for a big run, eat your preloading meal two days ahead of time instead of one.)

Urine test. A glance in the toilet after you relieve yourself is a good way to gauge whether or not you're well hydrated going into a run.

Your pee should be more clear than yellow. If your pee appears more like Gatorade than Crystal Light, drink more water before your run.

Measuring your sweat rate. Losing too much weight during a run is linked to a drop in blood volume, which can cause cramping and fatigue, among other problems. Knowing your sweat rate helps you plan roughly how much fluid you need on a run to avoid that weight loss. Here's how to measure it:

- Weigh yourself in the nude.

- Run for an hour without eating or drinking. *Run when temperatures and conditions are mild so that you won't get overly thirsty.*

- After your run, get naked.

- Towel off any sweat, urinate if you need to, and weigh yourself again.

If you've lost 2 pounds, you've lost a liter of fluids, and that's a lot. Know that you're a heavy sweater and need to bring and drink more fluids (than you might think) when you run.

Operator error

Internal troubles can wreak havoc on your body, ruin a run, and be detrimental to your health, depending on the severity. Knowing what ails you during your run—and acting wisely—can help you turn things around before they become more serious.

Bonk

What is it? A drop in muscle glycogen, blood glucose, or both due to insufficient fuel.

Signs. Fatigue, bad mood, headache, slowed pace, weakness, spaciness.

Deal with it. Ingest simple carbohydrates—also known as sugar.

Prevent it. Know approximately how many calories/hour your body needs while running. Ingest that much in various forms.

> Carbs in liquid form may be easier to stomach than solids during a bonk. They also go to work for your body quickly, helping to turn the bonk around.

FILTERING/TREATING WATER

On runs in areas where natural water exists in the form of a stream, river, lake, or snow, it may be tempting to kneel down and drink away.

Don't do it.

Especially at elevations where large animals roam, water sources can become contaminated with their feces. And still or slow-moving water plays host to all sorts of bacteria, other microorganisms (including giardia), and chemicals.

Following are some options for treating water on the trail.

Water treatment tablets. Iodine or chlorine dioxide tablets are small, inexpensive, and easy to drop into a water bottle or bladder. **DOWNSIDE:** Iodine takes 30 minutes to kill giardia and doesn't kill cryptosporidia (microscopic

It's safe to drink the water that comes out of a **natural spring** (usually a pipe) without filtering. You just need to know the location of the spring and judge your water needs and how long it will take you to reach it. Visit findaspring.com to see if there's one near you.

parasites that can cause diarrhea). Iodine also leaves an aftertaste. Chlorine dioxide tablets take 30 minutes to kill giardia and up to 4 hours to kill cryptosporidia.

Ultraviolet-light purifier. This nifty battery-powered light device zaps water with UV rays to ax bacteria, viruses, and other creepers. Water treatment takes less than a minute. **DOWNSIDE:** Requires batteries. *Bring extra batteries.*

Pump filter. A handheld filter made for backpacking works by pushing water through tiny pores and extracts bacteria and protozoa. **DOWNSIDE:** These filters don't kill or extract viruses (an issue near populated or agricultural areas) and are heavier and bulkier than other options. They take longer to manually filter than a UV purifier or iodine tablet (but you don't have to wait 30 minutes after treating).

> **THE DIRT** Seek out the fastest-flowing water you can find. The faster the water is moving over rocks and such, the more filtration it's undergone naturally.

 Add a **sports drink tablet** to water purified with iodine to combat the taste.

Filter, then treat with a virus-killing tablet if running in a populated or agricultural area.

 **WARNING**

Dehydration

What is it? A drop in blood volume due to insufficient liquids.

Signs. Cramping, fatigue, headache, nausea, weight loss.

Deal with it. Drink fluids, ideally with sodium.

Prevent it. Drink to your thirst. Check in with yourself regularly on a run to assess whether you're thirsty.

 **WARNING**

Hyponatremia

What is it? A low concentration of sodium in the blood, occurring through a combination of drinking too much water; sweating a lot; and not replacing lost **electrolytes** via sports drink, salty foods, or electrolyte capsules. The bloodstream becomes diluted, and sodium and potassium levels drop dangerously low. (Though rare, hyponatremia can be extremely dangerous.)

Signs. Puffiness, disorientation, headache, loss of energy, irritability, muscle weakness/spasms/cramps, seizures, coma.

electrolyte \e-'lek-truh-līt\ *n. (pl. -s)* 1. Substance that controls how our bodies absorb vitamins and minerals and process waste. 2. Substance lost during exercise that needs replacing—or else.

 For signs and treatment of **severe dehydration**, see "Internal Troubles," page 139.

Deal with it. Seek medical assistance immediately.

Prevent it. Alternate water with a sports drink, especially when it's hot outside and you're sweating buckets. Do not chug excessive amounts of plain water. The key is to not overhydrate.

> **TIP** If the taste of a sports drink is too concentrated for your liking, dilute by adding water to premixed drinks, adjusting powder amounts, or breaking tablets into halves or quarters. Just be aware that you're adjusting the amount of electrolytes and other contents when doing so.

Calories count

Making sure you ingest enough calories per hour while running can ensure that you don't run out of steam. Knowing a gel or three chews adds up to 100 calories helps you keep track of calories ingested in hopes of avoiding a bonk.

SAYS WHO

> "Food that enters into our stomachs is not ours yet. It needs to clear the stomach into the small intestine, be absorbed across the small intestine and go into the bloodstream, then it's yours. The more simple the carbohydrates, the quicker this happens."

SUNNY BLENDE, sports nutrition professor, owner of Eat4Fitness, veteran ultrarunner

PORTABLE FOOD THAT'S FAST FOOD!
FOOD ᴛᴏ GO

Eating during the run is a challenge, but options abound for small, convenient, portable packages of digestible energy.

FUEL

ENERGY GELS

Gooey, flavored concoctions in small, foil-like packets. Easy to digest and quick to convert to usable energy. Some have caffeine; most have electrolytes and other minerals useful to your body. Can be eaten one-handed (tear wrapper with teeth and suck).

Fine print: Can be sticky to eat. Can be even stickier afterward (wrapper is sticky and must not be discarded on the trail). Must ingest with water.

100

ENERGY CHEWS

Like gummy candy made out of energy fuel, usually the size of a large gumdrop. Easy to digest and quick to convert to usable energy. Less messy than gels. Some have caffeine; most have electrolytes and other minerals useful to your body.

Fine print: Bulkier to carry and harder to eat with one hand than gels.

Roughly 15 per chew
Packet of 6–12:

100 - 120

SPORT BEANS

Jelly beans formulated for sport with carbs, electrolytes, and vitamins. Some have caffeine. Come in a resealable bag.

Fine print: Can taste too sugary for those who don't like sugar. Harder to chew than energy chews.

Roughly 7 per bean
Packet of 15:

100

FUEL

ENERGY BARS

180-250°

Bar-shaped conglomerations formulated to fuel active endeavors. Come in a range of textures, sizes, flavors, ingredient mixes, and calorie counts. Can make you feel more full than gels or chews.

Fine print: Harder to cram into a pocket. Can be difficult to chew, swallow, and digest while running.

PROTEIN BARS

200-290

Bar-shaped conglomerations packed with 10 to 20 grams of protein, among other nutrients. (Some brands aimed at bodybuilders pack in up to 30 grams of protein.) Filling during a run and especially useful in helping muscles recover after a run.

Fine print: Harder to cram into a pocket. Harder to digest midrun than a regular bar, gels, or chews.

LIQUID CALORIES

Per 12 ounces:

40-160

Specially formulated powders mixed with water or premixed drinks provide calories and other dietary needs such as protein and minerals. Can be easier to digest than anything that needs to be chewed and provides some hydration benefits.

Fine print: Can be disgusting, like chugging milk midrun.

REAL FOOD

VARIES

Real food—such as nuts, dried fruit, pretzels, turkey sandwiches, or candy bars—tastes great on the trail, increasing the chance that you'll eat on your run.

Fine print: Real food isn't scientifically formulated specifically for endurance efforts. However, trial and error with the right foods can fuel you just fine.

 (non-protein-specific)

Portable Food That's Fast Food!

HYDRATION

WATER

0.00

Necessary for hydration—and life. Carrying water is increasingly necessary the longer you run. Water—in the form of a spring, creek, river, or lake—can be found along many trails but must be filtered or treated before drinking. (See "Filtering/Treating Water," page 90).

Fine print: Too much water and not enough electrolytes can be dangerous (see "Hyponatremia," page 92.) For those who ingest liquid only in the form of coffee, beer, or popsicles, water can taste boring. Carrying fluids adds weight.

SPORTS DRINKS

0.8–110 per 16 ounces,
Premixed liquid form:

VARIES

Powder/tablet form:

VARIES

Liquids formulated to support your body during exercise. Contain a mix of electrolytes and other minerals; some contain carbs. Come in several flavors, which can be refreshing during a run and encourage runners to keep drinking. Replenish electrolytes lost during exercise.

Fine print: Some replenish calories burned, while some have very few calories. Some contain sugar. If you tire of the flavor during a run, you might not want to drink; too much of a sugary sports drink can wreak havoc on your stomach and cause sores in your mouth. Read labels.

MIDRUN SUPPLEMENTS

ELECTROLYTE CAPSULES

0.00

Resembling a vitamin or magic bean, electrolyte capsules contain sodium and other minerals lost when you sweat. Small and lightweight, they are easy to carry and pop and are quick to take effect. Take with water.

Fine print: Pills can be hard to swallow on the run. Can't split a capsule pill in half. Doesn't taste yummy like a sports drink.

COMBOS/VALUE COMBOS

1 | The Classic
Choice of gel flavor

100

2 | The Medium Meal
Choice of flavors

220

3 | The Epic
Choice of flavors

1,000+

Why all the junk?

If you've ever seen an aid station at an ultramarathon, you've noticed that it is stocked with bowls of potato chips, M&Ms, cookies . . . with some bananas, orange slices, and soup. Wondering why the buffet is heavy on the "junk food"?

Ultrarunners exerting themselves for hours need to replenish their muscle glycogen and salt and need to up their caloric and hydration intakes to sustain themselves over time.

Muscle glycogen \'mə-səl 'glī-kə-jən\ *n.* 1. Main stored form of carbohydrates, necessary to make your muscles work and your body go.

Since running an ultramarathon can wreak havoc on taste buds and stomachs, aid stations present runners with an array of foods that might appeal to them. So, even if a runner feels as though he or she may barf, there's likely something on the table that they will at least attempt to ingest. If all else fails, a gel—also found at aid stations—may be the best option until the stomach settles.

The importance of protein

When eaten within 30 minutes of a run, protein helps repair muscle damage by allowing you to double-store glucose or glycogen in your muscle cells. That scientific function aids in recovery; you'll feel a lot better on your next run than you would if you didn't eat anything (or if you ate/drank just fries and a Coke).

Reloading

Reloading with fuel and liquid soon after finishing a run will help your body recover quickly so you don't feel crushed the rest of the day, or on your next run.

Quick protein:
- Chocolate milk (or regular milk)
- Protein bar or specifically formulated protein malt balls
- Protein drink mix and water
- Nuts, cheese, meats
- Beef, turkey, or other meat jerky

Necessary nutrients

Whether vegetarian, organic, gluten-free, or plain old meat and potatoes, there is not a one-size-fits-all diet plan for fueling a trail runner's body. The key is to fuel wisely and ensure that you are getting the nutrients you need. Some nutrients are more imperative than others. Here's the lowdown:

Carbohydrates. Your body burns carbohydrates as fuel. Real-food examples: Breads, pastas, rice, grains, fruits.

Proteins. Necessary for muscle repair. Real-food examples: Eggs, meats, nuts, dairy, beans, legumes.

Fats. Readily available as fuel for our bodies. Real-food examples: Good fats, such as the omega-3s found in walnuts, fish, flax, olive oil, coconut oil.

CARE AND FEEDING OF A TRAIL RUNNER

Trail runners, like all athletes, need to pay attention to what they put into their bodies if they want said bodies to perform. That said, trail runners are known to indulge in things such as whiskey and coffee (sometimes separately) and have a notable proclivity toward oversized burritos.

Vices: yes or no?

- **Coffee.** Coffee contains polyphenols known to be good for the brain, and caffeine has been proven to boost performance. Despite bad press, it has not been proven to be a diuretic.
- **Beer.** Malt and hops contain flavonoids, said to be good for your heart. Beer also contains vitamin B and chromium, which help convert carbs to energy.
- **Red wine.** Red wine contains resveratrol, which fights cholesterol. It also has flavonoids, which are good for your heart.
- **Chocolate.** Dark chocolate contains flavonols, which improve blood-vessel health. It is also known to improve skin health and lower cholesterol. Milk chocolate doesn't have the same amount of health benefits and has more refined sugar.

All of the above have negative effects when you ingest too much.

Electrolytes. Balance our sodium levels. Real-food examples: Broth, salted nuts, crackers, pickles.

Calcium. Needed for strong and healthy bones and to make muscles fire. Real-food examples: Milk, yogurt, cheese, soybeans, sardines.

Iron. The constant pounding of running leads to minute bleeding from tiny blood vessels, especially in our feet. We need iron to form new red blood cells and maintain energy levels. Real-food examples: Red meat, beans, spinach, poultry, raisins.

Vitamins. Needed for energy, metabolism, as antioxidants, to absorb other nutrients, and to promote healthy bones and tissues. Real-food examples: Broccoli, blueberries, nuts, carrots, potatoes, clams.

Water. Our bodies are made up mostly of water and need it to be constantly replenished in order to function properly. Real-food examples: Water.

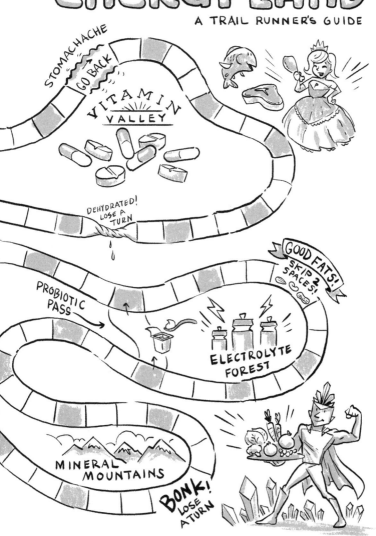

CHAPTER 7

Safety: Animals

Humans aren't the only creatures who like to play in the dirt. Running on trails almost guarantees you some interaction with wildlife, and that's a wonderful thing. Usually these encounters involve birds chirping, squirrels scurrying, and deer walking quietly with their fawns. The likelihood of a safe wildlife encounter is far greater than the likelihood of an unsafe wildlife encounter.

However, there is potential for a more exhilarating meeting with a predator, a snake, or any animal that feels a need to defend itself. Knowing what to do can keep these interactions positive.

predator \'pre-duh-ter, -tór\ n. (pl. -s) 1. An animal that eats other animals in order to live. 2. An animal that may occasionally confuse a human with food.

Critter encounters of the benign kind

What should you do when crossing paths with an animal? Look at them, even take a picture if—and this is key—you can do so from a safe distance. But generally, leave them be.

> ## SAFE INTERACTION 101
>
> **Don't feed.** No matter how much you think that squirrel wants to try your energy bar, don't feed it—or any other animal that larger animals like to eat, such as deer, mice, or chipmunks. More of the little guys means more of the bigger, toothier guys hanging around.
>
> **Don't pet.** Steer clear of cute baby predators. Their larger and very protective mothers are likely nearby, and a gentle animal can quickly turn into an angry animal.

Critter encounters of the potentially dangerous kind

As a trail runner, you're likely too lean and sinewy and, well, human, to appeal to a meat eater. That's not to say that there's no chance of danger. (Deer are lean, too.) Some animals are predators, after all, and challenging their territory—whether you mean to or not—could provoke some unpleasant natural instincts. No wild animal wants you messing with it, its young, or its personal space—so no close-talking or provoking these guys in any way. Here are some specifics on how to stay safe and defuse potentially unsafe situations in the wild.

This list is limited to critters that a runner might encounter in the United States. If running in other parts of the world, seek advice on what to do when face-to-face with local animals.

Dog

The most common animal encounter you'll likely have on a trail is with a dog running or hiking with a human. Dogs that are off leash should be well behaved and leave you alone, and the owner should be able to control the dog with a voice command. However, this is not always the case. If you are approaching a dog that appears agitated or is off leash and moving quickly in your direction, consider the following.

DO

- Greet the dog and owner with a friendly *hello*.
- Stay calm; dogs may become aggressive when sensing fear.
- Stop running and stand tall and still, like a tree.
- Stand sideways, keeping the dog in your peripheral vision. This is a less threatening stance to an aggressive dog.
- Lower your hand (with closed fist) so the dog can sniff you as it passes.
- Raise a knee to protect yourself should the dog jump up on you.

- Jump up and down excitedly.
- Stick out an open hand; this may too closely resemble a slice of ham.
- Freak out.
- Run away while freaking out. Running can trigger a chase instinct.

Coyote

These doglike creatures of the wild generally travel alone or in pairs but can sometimes be found in packs. They may entice their prey to follow them (*Let's go play!*) so that the pack can encircle said prey. Coyotes range between 20 and 50 pounds and eat rabbits, fish, frogs, rodents, deer, insects, snakes, fruit, grass, and sometimes livestock and small pets. They're most active from dusk to dawn.

There have been rare incidents of coyotes attacking runners and biting the backs of their legs and ankles. However, according to the Humane Society of the United States, more people are killed by errant golf balls or flying champagne corks than are bitten by coyotes. Nonetheless, caution is always a good thing.

DO

- Stay calm and back away slowly if you see the coyote and it doesn't see you.
- Stop running, stand tall, and yell if a coyote or pack of coyotes sees you and appears to be sizing you up.
- Throw something at the coyote(s). The goal is to scare it away, not hit it with a rock or stick.
- Make eye contact if the coyote is alone, and back away slowly. If it's a pack of coyotes, see "Do not."

- Turn your back on the animal and run away.
- Act threatening or look any of them in the eye if you are facing a pack.

Wolf

Wolves are typically afraid of humans. While you might run into a lone wolf (only in limited areas of the United States), they usually travel in packs. Both red and gray wolves are bigger than coyotes and behave a little differently. For one, they hunt bigger animals such as elk, deer, and moose. Wolves weigh between 40 (female red wolf) and 115 (male gray wolf) pounds and hunt day and night.

DO

- Sneak away quietly if you see a wolf before it sees you.
- Back away while facing the animal if it has seen you, making a space for it to escape and avoiding eye contact.
- Raise your voice and speak firmly.
- Wave your arms to look larger, yell, and throw things at the wolf if it acts aggressively.
- Fight back if attacked, trying to keep the wolf away from your head and neck.
- If attacked, go for its face. Its eyes and nose are sensitive.

DO NOT

- Look a wolf in the eye. They see it as a challenge.
- Run. You're not fast enough.
- If you are facing a pack, stand tall and appear aggressive.

Bobcat

Bobcats weigh roughly 15 to 35 pounds and are not to be confused with mountain lions, which are much larger. Bobcats are spotted and have short tails and tufted ears. They eat small animals such as rodents and rabbits. They're most active around sunrise and sunset.

DO

- Back away slowly.
- Make eye contact. This tells the bobcat you and your human eyes are not prey.
- Spray or squirt the bobcat with water, if possible.
- Make a lot of noise.
- Fight back if attacked.

DO NOT

- Run. This could trigger a pursuit.

Mountain lion

Mountain lions weigh between 80 and 180 pounds and are typically 5 to 8 feet long, nose to tail. They have a long tail with a dark tip and are uniformly tan or grayish in color. Mountain lions prey on large and small mammals such as deer, raccoons, and beaver and are most active at dawn and dusk.

DO

- Stop running and face the lion.
- Make eye contact.

Mountain lions are also referred to as pumas, panthers, catamounts, and cougars.

- Make yourself appear as big as possible. Raise your arms, open your jacket, and stand close to your running partner. Wave your raised arms slowly.
- Make noise by yelling and banging rocks together.
- Speak slowly and firmly in a deep voice.
- Throw something you have in your hands (don't bend or crouch down).
- Back away slowly. If you're between the lion and its prey or kittens, give the lion a path to get to its treasure.
- Fight back if attacked, protecting your throat and neck.

DO NOT
- Bend or crouch down.
- Turn your back and run. Mountain lions like a good game of chase, and they win by pouncing on the slower playmate.

Bear

Of the few species of bears that roam the continent, black bears (which range in color from black to brown or even white) are the ones you're most likely to encounter on a trail run in the United States. They live in most forested regions of the country as well as in mountainous and swampy areas.

Grizzly bears, including coastal brown bears, range from black to blond and live in the northern reaches of the country (Alaska, Montana, Idaho, Washington, Wyoming, and western Canada). Grizzlies roam inland.

Both kinds of bears hibernate but have been known to come out of their dens in the winter. And though they're more active at dawn and dusk, they can be out and about at any hour.

THE DIRT Bears can be active for up to 20 hours a day in the fall. It's a phase called "hyperphagia"—the time of year when they eat and drink excessively before hibernation season.

Who am I? Grizzlies are generally larger than black bears; however, there are large black bears and small grizzlies. How do you tell black and grizzly bears apart? And do you need to know the difference? Only if you like identifying animals. Your response to any bear encounter should depend on the circumstances and the bear's behavior, not on the species.

Black Bears

Grizzly Bears

Black Bears:
- Larger, rounded ears
- No shoulder hump
- Straight face profile
- Smaller claws

Grizzly Bears:
- Concave facial profile
- Smaller, rounded ears
- Pronounced shoulder hump
- Larger claws

Running in bear country. Most bears are afraid of or uninterested in humans. However, a threatened bear, or the very rare predatory bear, can become a serious issue.

DO

- Carry bear spray® where you can grab it quickly (not on your back).
- Read bear spray instructions beforehand—spray duration and distance vary among brands.
- Start to spray a charging bear when it is 30 to 60 feet away.

Encounter #1: You see a bear and it doesn't see you.

- Stay calm.
- Back away slowly.

Encounter #2: A bear sees you.

- Stay calm.
- Talk in quiet tones, telling the bear you're a human.
- If the bear returns to doing bear things, back away slowly, as you would if the bear had never seen you.

Encounter #3: A bear sees you and charges.

- Stand your ground. (The charge may be a bluff.)
- Use your bear spray.

Encounter #4: A bear charges and makes contact.

- Drop to the ground and play dead by covering the back of your neck with your hands and protecting your face with your forearms, elbows on the ground.

Carry EPA-approved **bear spray** as your bear deterrent. Don't depend on personal defense products such as pepper spray to stop a charging bear.

- Play dead for longer than you think you need to. A bear may sniff you or simply watch you to make sure you are no longer a threat before leaving. If you move too early, you'll likely regain its attention.

Encounter #5: A bear is stalking you.
- A predatory bear will be intent and focused on you. It will approach you with its head up and ears erect. If you think a bear is following you, make a 90-degree turn and walk 100 to 300 yards, make another 90-degree turn, and walk another 100 to 300 yards, and so on. It may just be curious and leave you alone once its curiosity is satisfied.
- Be aggressive toward the bear from the get-go: Talk loudly, wave your arms, look as big as possible, and throw things, showing the bear that you are not easy prey while you walk and turn, walk and turn.

An encounter with a predatory bear is extremely rare, but knowing how to react is important.

SAYS WHO

"Trail running in grizzly country is not recommended because of the increased risk of a surprise encounter and the danger that poses for the runner and the bear."

KATE WILMOT, bear management specialist for Grand Teton National Park

THE DIRT Although black bears are better climbers than grizzly bears, they both can climb better than humans, which means that climbing a tree is not a safe option.

RULE of THUMB Since off-leash dogs can attract grizzlies and lure them back to their owners, it's a good idea to keep dogs on leash in grizzly country, even when walking.

Moose

Moose are large animals, and the males (called "bulls") have paddle-like antlers. They are not particularly interested in humans, but if a moose feels threatened or is trying to protect its calf, it may charge. (It's the hooves you need to worry about, not the antlers.) Moose are herbivores, eating only plants. They weigh between 900 and 1,500 pounds and are most active at dawn and dusk.

THE DIRT The plural of moose is not "mooses" or "meese." It's "moose," as in *Good thing I've been doing speed work because I had to run away from two moose today!*

- Give a moose space.
- Keep your dog under control.
- Look for warning signs. If a moose begins moving its ears, raising its hair, smacking its lips, bulging its eyes, tossing its head, or urinating, it's warning you. Give it even more space.
- Run if it charges. Moose sometimes drop their pursuit after a few strides.
- Try to get a tree between you and the moose while you run. (Most moose attacks are bluffs, and the tree will deter them.)
- Get up and keep running if the moose knocks you down.

DO NOT

- Stand your ground. Just get the heck out of there.
- Think you're scot-free if you can jump into a body of water. Moose are very good swimmers. (But then again, they likely won't pursue you.)

Elk

Elk, like moose, are large animals with antlers (the males), but the elk's antlers are thinner than those of a moose. Elk can weigh up to 700 pounds and are found mostly in the western United States. Elk are light brown and cream, and their necks are usually darker than the rest of their bodies. They are herbivores, eating only plants.

DO

- Give an elk space.
- Run quickly to the other side of something, such as a fence or tree, that will block its path if it charges.
- Get up and keep running if the elk knocks you down.

- Stand your ground. Just get the heck out of there.
- Think you're totally safe if you can jump into a body of water. Elk are very good swimmers. (But they likely won't pursue you. They are not predators.)

Bison

Found on prairies around the United States (and in the woodlands of western Canada), where they eat grasses and other plants, bison can weigh more than 2,000 pounds and run up to 40 mph. That means you don't want to mess with a bison.

DO

- Give bison space.
- Hide behind anything you can. They're less likely to detect (and care about) stationary objects than moving ones.

DO NOT

- Startle them with loud noises or sudden movement.
- Annoy them by approaching.

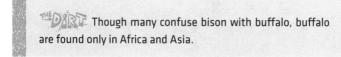

THE DIRT Though many confuse bison with buffalo, buffalo are found only in Africa and Asia.

Deer

Deer are ever-present in the wild and in nearly all cases are docile and safe. There have been rare instances of humans being gored by buck antlers or stomped. In those cases, the buck was likely startled by the human or accompanying dog. Deer are herbivores and can weigh up to 300 pounds.

DO

- Make your presence known by making noise, calmly.
- Run away.
- Climb a tree.
- Play dead if attacked.

DO NOT

- Sneak up on or scare deer.

HUNTING SEASON!

To stay safe on the trails during hunting season, follow these tips:

- **Know the season and the trails.** Look online for hunting seasons and where hunting is allowed in your area, and consider changing your running location while the hunters are out. Read trail signs for allowed activities in addition to looking online before you go.
- **Avoid dusk and dawn.** Since the hunted are most active at dusk and dawn, so are the hunters. Running in the middle of the day is safer (though not necessarily hunter-free).
- **Dress in bright colors.** To be seen by hunters, wear vivid running clothing—a bright-orange hat or shirt, for instance.

Bull

Bulls are generally kept behind secure barbed-wire farm fences. They're ridiculously fast, can turn on a dime, and are pretty smart. Only if you're in Pamplona should you consider running with a bull, and even then . . . These animals weigh upward of 3,300 pounds.

DO

- Stay far away from a bull.
- Throw something if a bull charges—a pack, water bottle, loose clothing—to distract it.
- Run to the nearest thing that will separate you from the bull: a fence, gate, or cattle guard. Bulls are fast, so make it a short run, and make it quick.
- Climb a nearby tree if there's one sturdy enough to hold you.
- Stand your ground and fight if all else fails. Yell at the bull or punch it in the nose.

DO NOT

- Taunt a bull by challenging, teasing, or aggravating it. Certainly do not wave a cape.
- Stand still for more than a second with a mad bull staring you down.

Cow

Some trails cut through areas where cows freely feed. Cows may seem like ridiculous animals to fear, but they are big, weighing up to 1,000 pounds, and can become agitated if provoked. Cows gen-

---

 Bulls aren't particularly drawn to the red color of a **matador's cape**. It's the tantalizing movement of the cape that attracts their attention.

erally have little interest in humans and are not aggressive. But an angry cow is a potential danger.

- Avoid walking through a herd of cows.
- Talk calmly to the cows if you must walk through the herd, encouraging them to move out of your way.
- Walk quietly and quickly.
- Punch a cow in the nose if she attacks.

- Go near a calf. Mama cows are protective.
- Make eye contact.
- Appear aggressive by making loud sounds or waving your arms. This irritates cows, and an irritated cow is a dangerous cow.
- Second-guess your instincts. If a cow looks irritated, it probably is.

Wild pig/boar

Found largely in Texas, Hawaii, and sporadically in other parts of the United States, wild pigs and boar can be aggressive when provoked. They have large, hard heads; the males have tusks that they use for protection; and they can run up to 30 mph.

 THE DIRT All boar are pigs, but not all pigs are boar.

- Stop running.
- Back away slowly, talking calmly to the animal.

- Provoke the pig or boar.
- Get too close.
- Yell or act aggressively in any way.

Goose

Canada geese, found in both Canada and the United States, are the most aggressive type of wild geese, but other species can be persnickety as well. Geese are very protective of themselves and their young. When they feel threatened, they hiss and approach humans. They've been known to peck and bite. Canada geese have black heads and necks with white patches on their faces. Other types of geese are either white, grey, or black.

DO

- Give geese plenty of space.
- Run away.

DO NOT

- Crowd their personal space.
- Try to pet geese or goslings.
- Stand your ground.

Animal Action Plan

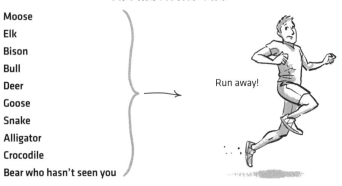

Moose	
Elk	
Bison	
Bull	
Deer	Run away!
Goose	
Snake	
Alligator	
Crocodile	
Bear who hasn't seen you	

Mad dog	
Coyote	
Wolf	Stand tall
Bobcat	then back
Mountain lion	away slowly
Wild pig	
Bear who has seen you	

Reptiles
Snake

Roughly 100 types of snakes slither around the United States, most of them nonvenomous and essentially harmless. However, there are 20 species of venomous snakes in the U.S.: 16 types of rattlesnakes, 2 types of coral snakes, and the cottonmouth (also known as "water moccasin"). Coral snakes have the most potent venom.

These cold-blooded creatures like to warm themselves in sunny places on sunny days. When it's hot, they cool themselves

 Walk quickly past **cows**.

in the shade. Their most active period is spring through early fall. They are nocturnal hunters, spending the day resting and sunning themselves. Depending on the type of snake, they eat small rodents, birds, fish, frogs, and insects.

If you come across a snake, knowing what type it is can be a potential lifesaver should you get bitten. Informing medical professionals about the snake that struck you helps them quickly administer the proper treatment.

Rattlesnakes. Rattlesnakes are common all over the continental United States, especially in the Southwest. They're between 1 and 8 feet long, with bulky bodies and catlike pupils with no eyelids. Their heads are triangular, wide at the neck, and they have a pit between their eyes and nostrils (a distinguishing feature of a pit viper). They can be brown, gray, rust, yellow, cream, beige, and of various patterns.

The most distinguishing rattlesnake feature is the rattle at the end of their tails, but know that rattles sometimes fall off.

Cottonmouth snakes. Also known as water moccasins, these reptiles live in the southeastern United States, including eastern Texas. They can be up to 4 feet long and have large, triangular heads with pits between their eyes and nostrils (they are a type of pit viper, like rattlesnakes). Their bulky bodies taper to a narrow tail and are dark brown or dull black with lighter banding. When a cottonmouth opens its mouths in aggression, the sticky "spit" looks as if it just woke up after a bender and needs a Big Gulp.

Coral snakes. These are the most lethal snakes in the U.S. but look an awful lot like the less dangerous scarlet king snake. Keep this rhyme in mind:

Florida **DRIVER LICENSE**   **USA**

CLASS: REPTILE

NAME:

CORAL SNAKE

COLOR: **RED, YELLOW AND BLACK RINGS (RED AND YELLOW TOUCHING)**

NOSE: **BLACK**
LENGTH: 18-30 INCHES

Coral Snake

FLORIDA: **DRIVER LISENCE**   **USA**

CLASS: REPTILE

NAME:

Scarlett king snake

AKA: "THE MASTER MIMIC"

COLOR: RED BLACK AND YELLOW RINGS (BLACK AND YELLOW TOUCHING)

NOSE: RED
LENGTH: 40-50 CM

SCARLETT K. SNAKE

> *Red touch yellow—kill a fellow*
> *Red touch black—venom lack*

Regardless of the type of snake you encounter on the trail, your actions should be the same.

DO
- Leave the snake alone.
- Give it a wide berth.
- Back away calmly as quickly and quietly as you can.

DO NOT
- Stick your hands in crevices.
- Sit on logs or craggy rocks without looking around them and inside.
- Step over a log into a shady, possible snake-napping spot.
- Provoke the snake in any way.

RULE **—of— THUMB** If struck by a snake, stay calm and seek medical help as soon as possible. For more on what to do (and not to do), see "Snakebite," page 144.

Alligator/crocodile

Alligators have wide, rounded snouts, while crocodiles have long, narrow, pointier snouts. Crocodiles' teeth overlap and stick out of their mouths; alligators' do not. Both are found in the southern United States—alligators mostly in freshwater and crocodiles in salty or muddy waters. Both defend their territory like hungry runners defending their last gel or postrun beer, especially during mating season—April through July for alligators and July and August for crocodiles.

DO

- Keep your distance from shorelines to minimize encounters.
- Give it a wide berth (at least 15 feet).
- Run (away from the water).
- Fight back if attacked. Go for the eyes, the nostrils, the ears, the palatal valve (a valve behind the tongue). If your arm is in its mouth, push on that valve, and it will likely let go.

DO NOT

- Jump into a pond and try to swim away from a crocodile or alligator.
- Run in a zigzag pattern; this is an old myth. Instead, run straight as fast as you can.

Insects

Interactions with insects can be pleasant; think butterflies fluttering. There are, however, places and times of the year where bugs can be a nuisance and even a health issue. When the nuisance goes beyond grasshoppers bumping into your legs with every step and elevates to mosquitoes attacking, you'll want to cover as much skin as possible and coat yourself with a safe bug repellent.

When the bug-human interaction becomes ticks latching or bees or wasps stinging, proper treatment makes a difference (see "Stings and Bites," page 141).

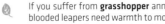 If you suffer from **grasshopper** annoyance, run when it's coolest, as these cold-blooded leapers need warmth to move. Grasshoppers frequent dry areas with tall grass but also live in forests and jungles.

Tracking tracks

Spotting tracks on the trail will alert you to what's recently been in the area. Some tracks should make you turn around and run the other way. Others simply heighten your awareness and prepare you for a possible encounter.

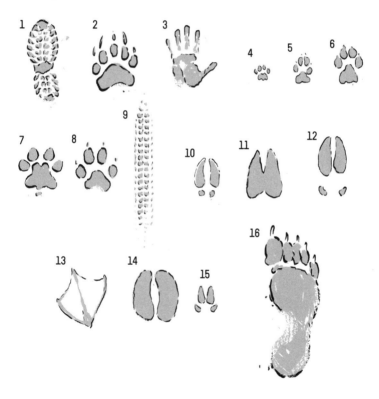

CHAPTER 8

Safety: First Aid

Like most sports, trail running is an activity with the potential for injury: Twist an ankle, skin a knee, swallow a bug. And there may be poison oak, stinging nettles, or snakes. Never fear. Trail runners are a crafty, self-sufficient lot, which is good because getting help midrun isn't as easy as it is on a road run.

Ideally, you'd always carry a first-aid kit and know exactly how to use it. (See "First Aid Lite," page 57.) But in reality, you'll likely head out for your runs with a phone and possibly some water. Or maybe with nothing at all.

Since knowledge is the real power, and doesn't require much gear, read on.

Common injuries

Trails can be riddled with obstacles—roots, ruts, and rocks—providing a natural playground to navigate. However, these can

also send you sprawling. Some trail injuries happen in the blink of an eye, making you wish you could rewind time for 1 second so you could avoid a certain rock and not twist your ankle or skin your knee (see "Technically Sound," page 216). Time travel is impossible, but knowing what to do when injuries happen is not.

Sprained ankle

Challenging your muscles, ligaments, and bones with uneven terrain strengthens your ankles and everything around them. The more you trail run, the sturdier you become. However, unforeseen dips or unexpected obstacles can surprise even the savviest runner.

Deal with it. If you sprain an ankle on the trail and are able to bear weight on it, make your way back to the trailhead. Once you have access to ice, a treatment of R.I.C.E. (rest, ice, compression, elevation) may help minimize pain and swelling.

While the **R.I.C.E.** treatment doesn't do any harm and may do lots of good, the jury is out in the world of sports medicine regarding its tangible effectiveness.

THE DIRT If you sprain or twist an ankle on the trail, running or walking through the pain to get home won't injure you more. In fact, moving keeps blood flowing and prevents the joint from stiffening up. What might injure you, however, is twisting it again since the injured ankle is unstable.

AN OUNCE OF PREVENTION . . .

Strengthening your ankles can be a preventive measure for sprains. Try the following while sitting at your desk or on the couch. Pretend that you're writing the alphabet in the air with your foot.

ABCs

What you need. Bare feet and a basic knowledge of the alphabet.

For more on ankle strengthening, see "Home Improvement," page 202.

It is best to stay off an injured ankle until inflamma-
tion and pain subside. If the sprain is mild and you
choose to continue running on it, tape it for support by using
three J-shaped strips around the ankle and a couple of straps
around your lower leg, wrapping around the J-strips.

Fractured bone

Bones can fracture or break in a twist or a fall. It's also possible to acquire a stress fracture, which sometimes happens with time and use. Fractures and breaks are sensitive to the touch and should be assessed by medical professionals.

Deal with it. Signs that a bone may be broken include a snapping or grinding noise upon injury (aside from stress fractures, which are sound-free), swelling, and/or deformity of the limb. If you think a bone is broken, see a doctor for an x-ray, an evaluation, and a treatment plan.

Tweaked knee

Running trails gives knees a break, as compared with the harsher pounding on road pavement. However, knees can still be tweaked—strained, twisted, or even sprained. In a strain, the muscles or tendons are compromised. A twist puts stress on the cartilage or meniscus, causing potential tears. A sprain is a stretch or tear of the ligaments.

 To **minimize trip-ups** by improving your technical running skills, see "Technically Sound," page 216.

"Tweaked" knees—in the general sense—can also result from imbalances, tightness, or weakness built up over time. (See "Mystery Aches and Pains," page 159.)

Deal with it. Hobble back to your car or house, apply R.I.C.E., and seek medical advice if pain persists.

Stubbed toe

Accidentally kicking a rock, root, or log can make you scream a word not suitable for children's ears. Luckily, most trail running shoes have protective toe bumpers made of more durable materials than the rest of the upper to help ease the blow.

Most stubbed toes heal quickly. However, should you suffer ongoing pain for several days, you may want to see a doctor to rule out a cracked, chipped, or broken bone. Be warned: A toenail may turn black from the blow, but don't panic; it'll likely fall off on its own without any serious repercussions.

Deal with it. Curse loudly if you need to, and keep running. Check the toe when you get home, and treat any black toenails with the advice on page 138 ("Black Toenails").

Abrasions

Cuts and scrapes happen occasionally, especially if you're prone to tripping on rocks or find yourself bushwhacking through prickly

Long shoelaces can trip you up or get snagged on low branches. Tie double knots to shorten laces. If your shoes have one-pull laces, tuck the excess into the "lace garage" (a pocket sewn into the top of the tongue of some shoes) or into a loop somewhere along the lace line.

shrubs and sharp branches. In fact, abrasions can be badges of honor. The main concern for an abrasion or a laceration incurred on a trail is avoiding infection.

HOW TO: Treat an Abrasion

- Squirt water on the cut to remove visible trail debris.
- If you have a bandage or gauze, cover the wound to keep it free of further debris.
- Once home, clean thoroughly with soap and water or topical wound antiseptic.
- Remove all remnants of nature from your skin, using tweezers if needed.
- Clean again.
- Cover with a fresh bandage or gauze and tape when going to bed at night to avoid sticking to sheets.

Bleeding

Trail falls happen; ergo, so do trail cuts. And cuts bleed—some more than others, depending on where they occur on the body and how deeply you gouge yourself. Remember that the depth of a cut is generally more of a concern than the length.

HOW TO: Get a Cut to Stop Bleeding

- Apply pressure to the wound with a bandage, a clean cloth, or the cleanest part of what you're wearing.

- Continue pressure. If you have tape or other means of keeping pressure on the bleeding spot (for example, wrapping it in a sock or taping it with athletic tape), do so. If not, continue to apply pressure with your hand.

- Raise it. Elevating the bleeding wound above the heart helps slow bleeding.

RULE of **THUMB** Do not apply direct pressure to an eye injury or to a bleeding wound with something embedded in it.

Head injury

As opposed to a fueling bonk (see "Bonk," page 89), a bonked head can happen to a trail runner who's paying too much attention to their footing to notice the low branch she or he should have ducked under.

Smacking your head hard into an overhanging object or on the ground, a log, or a rock can pose a serious concern. If you have a persistent headache, experience nausea or vomiting, or black out, seek medical help.

TIP If running in a forested area with low-hanging tree branches, remove your cap or visor while running. Wearing a bill over your eyes increases the chances of obstacles at head height sneaking up on you.

Blisters

What starts off as an annoying hot spot in your shoe can quickly turn into a liquid-filled blister. Blisters are your body's way of padding and protecting your skin from a rub, and if ignored, they can turn into a shredded and flapping exterior layer of skin with painfully exposed raw skin underneath. The key is treating a hot spot before it turns into a blister.

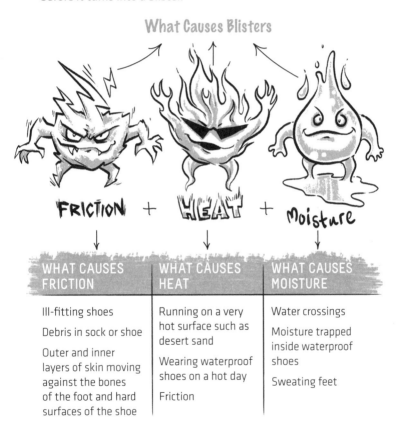

What Causes Blisters

FRICTION + HEAT + Moisture

WHAT CAUSES FRICTION	WHAT CAUSES HEAT	WHAT CAUSES MOISTURE
Ill-fitting shoes	Running on a very hot surface such as desert sand	Water crossings
Debris in sock or shoe		Moisture trapped inside waterproof shoes
Outer and inner layers of skin moving against the bones of the foot and hard surfaces of the shoe	Wearing waterproof shoes on a hot day	Sweating feet
	Friction	

HOW TO: Treat a Blister

If a hot spot turns into a blister during a run, consider stopping to treat it before it ruptures and causes more pain.

- Remove your shoe and sock.

- Place an adhesive bandage or gauze secured with duct tape over the blister, taking care to keep the tape or bandage wrinkle-free. Or try foil packaging from a gel or soft leaves layered between the irritation and your sock.

Alternatively, you can pop the blister using use a small, sterile needle. To do so, make a few small puncture holes on the edges of the blister, stretching the skin from side to side to enlarge the hole and keep it from sealing up on itself.

- Press gently on the blister, expelling as much fluid as possible.

- Clean the area with an antiseptic.

- Cover with gauze and athletic tape, duct tape, or blister pads (or leaves or foil if necessary).

Duct tape \duhkt teyp\ n. 1. Sticky silver cloth tape. 2. Possibly the best MacGyverlike material ever invented.

"While it's better to get the fluid out rather than let the blister get larger, using anything non-sterile to lance a blister could cause an infection."

JOHN VONHOF, author of *Fixing Your Feet*

Black toenails

Trail runners, especially ultrarunners, are not known for pretty toes. A common affliction is black toenails caused by extensive downhill running, too-tight shoes, or many miles on the trail. The underside of toenails can fill with blood, like a bruise, and when that blood dries, it becomes black. When a toenail is black, it usually falls off in a few weeks, and a new toenail grows back. To prevent black toenails, keep toenails short and filed smooth, and make sure your shoes fit comfortably, especially when running downhill. If your toes are hitting the front of your shoe, the shoe is too small or otherwise ill-fitting. Size up, and/or try a different model.

Black toenails can be painful due to the buildup of pressure beneath the nail. This will resolve itself over time. There is a way to alleviate the pain immediately, but it is only for the brave.

HOW TO: Deal with Painful Black Toenails

- Clean the area with soap and water, and wipe it down with antiseptic.

- Heat the end of a needle over a flame to sterilize it and to get it hot enough to puncture your nail.

- Make a drain hole. If the edge of a blister can be seen under the toenail edge, make the drain hole there. If no blister is visible at the edge, slowly poke the needle through your nail to relieve pressure. Squeeze the nail downward to let blood drain out.

THE DIRT Some dedicated ultramarathoners have been known to have all their toenails removed in order to avoid toenail issues altogether.

- Clean the area again, and wrap it with gauze and tape or large bandages.
- Tell your friends about it—especially squeamish friends.

Internal troubles

Some ailments on the trail are not the fault of the terrain or how you negotiate it. A range of variables, such as a questionable breakfast choice or lack of fluid intake, combined with intense pace or crazy heat can cause internal upheaval. Knowing the signs can help keep troubles at bay.

CHECK YO SELF®

SYMPTOMS	AILMENT & ACTION
Fatigue, bad mood, weakness, headache, slowed pace, gastrointestinal distress	**Bonk!** Ingest simple sugars, such as a gel, until you feel well enough to ingest more calories.
Dry mouth, thirst, infrequent urination, dry skin, headache, constipation, dizziness, gastrointestinal distress	**Dehydration!** Drink when thirsty, including electrolytes.
Extreme thirst, extremely dry mouth, infrequent urination, dark urine, sunken eyes, shriveled skin, low blood pressure, rapid heartbeat, fever, delirium	**Severe dehydration!** Drink, and seek medical help.
Nausea, vomiting, headache, confusion, extreme fatigue, irritability, muscle weakness, spasms or cramps, seizures	**Hyponatremia!** Stop drinking water, then take sodium. Seek medical assistance—quickly.

 For the scoop on bonking, dehydration, and hyponatremia, see "Operator Error," page 898.

Gastrointestinal distress

Gastrointestinal (GI) issues are no fun, even when you're not on a run. But they are truly an antiparty when you are miles from a toilet. Causes can include dehydration, bonking, not enough blood flow to the internal organs, and more. To try to identify the culprit, consider keeping a log about your diet, time of run, weather, and the severity of the situation. This may help you home in on the problem and avoid it on future runs. If the problem is ongoing, see a doctor.

 TIP Carry toilet paper or wet wipes, sealed in a plastic baggy for easy "leave no trace" carry-out.

For the scoop on the environmentally and socially ethical way to handle GI distress on a run, see "How to: Poop in the Woods," page 177.

Muscle cramps

Muscles cramping during a run can be debilitating. Cramps have a range of causes, from poor nutrition and hydration to muscle weaknesses and/or imbalances that cause spasms to not allowing muscles to recover enough from a tough workout before heading out again.

Deal with it. Try massaging out the cramp (note: stretching can make it worse). Hydrate with electrolytes. Eat. Rest. Seek medical advice if a cramp persists. For a long-term solution, develop a prevention strategy based on why you got the cramp in the first place.

Stings and bites

Don't let insects or other small critters bug you. Interactions can be as pleasant as hopping over a caterpillar or spotting a firefly. However, once in a while, an encounter can be, well, a buzzkill.

Bees and wasps

Bees are generally harmless creatures going about their pollenating, honey-making ways, but occasionally they sting. This can happen if a bee gets trapped in your clothing or if you sit down in an unlucky spot.

Wasps also sting and are more aggressive than bees.

Bee and wasp stings hurt and cause some itching and swelling. If you think you're having a severe allergic reaction, head straight to an emergency room for treatment. If you already know you are allergic, you should run carrying an EpiPen prescribed by a doctor.

 Bees (not wasps) may leave their stingers in your skin with the venom sack still attached. If possible, remove the stinger as quickly as possible with a sharp fingernail, tweezers, or a credit card.

Ticks

A variety of ticks live in tall grasses across the United States, and some carry pathogens for ailments such as Lyme disease and Rocky Mountain spotted fever. Always check your skin after a trail run, particularly if you ran through tall grass. If you find that a tick has latched on to you, remove it promptly and properly.

HOW TO: Remove a Tick

- Use fine-tipped tweezers or extrafine tick forceps (found at a medical supply store or online retailer).

- Reach just below the tick's head to grab the parts of the head latched on to your skin.

- Pull in one straight movement up and out. Do not squish the body of the tick, which could squeeze more pathogens into your bloodstream.

- Sterilize your skin with rubbing alcohol or other sterilizer.

- Keep the tick for reference in a clear plastic bag in case you develop symptoms of illness.

Leeches

In North America, leeches are found in lakes, ponds, marshes—the weedier, the better—mud, and slow-moving streams and sometimes latch on to humans during water crossings. They can be found across the United States, most commonly around the Great Lakes. The good news is that, unlike mosquitoes and ticks, leeches aren't known to transmit diseases to humans. If you find a leech latched on to you, remove it, and don't be alarmed if the area bleeds for a couple of days.

HOW TO: Remove a Leech

- Use a fingernail, credit card, or other flat, hard-edged object to scrape along the attachment site on one end of the leech.

- Repeat on the other end of the leech.

- Flick the leech away from you. Scream.

- Clean the sucked area with soap and water, and cover it with a bandage.

Mosquitoes

Most mosquito bites are merely annoying, itchy lumps on your skin. However, mosquitoes can transmit diseases such as West Nile virus and even malaria. If you live and run in a buggy area, consider wearing long sleeves and pants and using insect repellent.

One in five people inflicted with **West Nile virus** has symptoms, and 99 percent of the people who do suffer flulike symptoms recover completely.

Deal with it. Try not to scratch a mosquito bite so much that you break the skin, which could become infected. Try slapping it instead. If you develop flulike symptoms (achiness, fever) following a mosquito bite, seek medical advice.

Swallowing a bug

Swallowing a bug when running is more common than you might think. After all, you're sharing the same space. A swallowed bug will take one of two paths: down your esophagus and into your stomach or down your windpipe and into your lungs. A bug that travels into your stomach simply gets digested. A bug that travels into your lungs may cause an inflammatory reaction in your throat and lungs for a few days.

Deal with it. Cough, spit, or gag to get the bug out of your mouth. If it is lodged too far back in your throat, try to swallow it. Water will help. If discomfort persists, see a doctor.

Snakebite

It happens rarely, but it happens. Knowing what to do if bitten by a snake makes a big difference in recovery. The old advice of making a tourniquet out of a tube sock or hair band has been thrown out the window.

HOW TO: Deal with a Snakebite

Most importantly, stay calm. While this may be difficult, panicking increases blood flow, which spreads venom. Remind yourself that one-third of snakebites don't inflict venom.

DO

- Remain calm.
- Note the size, color, and head shape of the snake in order to help identify it to a medical professional. However, do not waste time looking for it. It's more important to seek help quickly.
- Circle the bite area with a pen if you have one, and note the time and description of the snake.
- Remove any jewelry before swelling starts.
- Go to a hospital emergency room immediately.

DON'T

- Panic. Increased blood flow due to panic spreads venom.
- Use a tourniquet to restrict the area.
- Try to cut out the bitten area or try to suck out the venom.
- Sit or lie down and wait for help.
- Use ice.

"Ideally, you don't move when struck by a snake. You stay calm and flat and somebody magically transports you to the doctor. The practical side is that people may have to walk. Try to get your brain to accept the rationality that a third of bites don't invenomate. And the ones that do—know that most adults can tolerate the venom."

TOD SCHIMELPFENIG, curriculum director for National Outdoor Leadership School Wilderness Medicine Institute

Information about the snake and the incident may help a medical professional treat you. However, it's more important to get to a medical facility than to spend time taking notes on yourself.

Mammal bites

If you are bitten by an animal on the trail, clean any puncture wounds to prevent infection. Some animals—dogs, cats, skunks, raccoons, bats, foxes, coyotes, rodents, rabbits, hares, pikas—have the potential to carry rabies or other diseases.

If you've had a tetanus shot and the animal doesn't have rabies, you should be fine. If neither of these things is true, or you do not know whether or not the animal that bit you is rabid, seek medical help. If the wound shows sign of infection, seek medical attention.

Plant-inflicted hazards

Over the river and through the woods might take you through rash-inducing or prickly plants. Know how to identify which plants to avoid.

| Poison oak | Poison ivy | Sumac |

"Leaves of three, let it be"

If you see poison oak, poison ivy, or sumac, avoid contact. If you run somewhere rife with any of the plants, wear long sleeves and long pants or tights. If it's shorts and short-sleeves weather, opt for long socks and arm warmers/coolers (see "Conditional Love," page 58) to minimize bare skin.

If you do make contact with a poisonous plant, take preventive measures to try to abate the itchy rash.

HOW TO: Lessen or Avoid a Rash from Toxic Plant Oils

- Scrub your skin postrun with a skin cleanser specifically formulated to remove a plant's urushiol oils (See "Poisonous Plants," page 66). The sooner the better—and the longer you scrub, the better. If no oak, ivy, and sumac cleanser is available, scrub with dishwashing soap or rubbing alcohol.

- Rinse off in **hot** water, using more oil-removing soap. (Hot water is more effective than cold for removing the oil.)

- Wash a few hours later with more urushiol oil–removing solution or dish soap and hot water.

- Wash all clothes and shoes (wearing gloves to handle them) that came into contact with the oak, ivy, or sumac. Regular detergent and hot water should remove all oils.

- Wash your dog (wearing gloves) with an oil-removing solution if he or she came into contact with the plants.

 Poison **sumac plants** can have leaves of 7 to 13.

HOW TO: Pacify an Itchy Rash

- Wash frequently with a rash-specific scrub.

- Apply anti-itch lotion.

- Apply rubbing alcohol and acne treatment cleansing pads (which dry the rash area).

- Take scalding-hot showers or blow warm air from a hair drier over the affected area to provide an hour or two of relief from itching.

- Chlorine in a pool or hot tub may help dry out the rash.

- Don't scratch. If you can't resist scratching, avoid tearing the skin. Try patting vigorously or wearing socks over your hands to cover your nails.

- A steroid shot may be administered by a physician if needed.

⚡ **BAD** NEWS A hot shower without soap spreads poison oak, ivy, and sumac oils. Don't do it!

☀ **GOOD** NEWS A hot shower with soap, urushiol-specific soap, or dishwashing soap helps remove oils. Do it!

 Be ready for **stares** from your fellow pool/hot-tub users. Do you blame them?

 If you have any **systemic reactions** to being exposed to poison oak, poison ivy, or sumac—difficulty breathing, for instance—seek medical help immediately.

Stinging and burning nettles

Nettle is found in 49 of the 50 U.S. states (Florida is nettle-free!) and throughout Canada and Mexico. Stinging-nettle plants are found in meadows, marshes, and moist forests, and burning nettles are found mainly near coastlines. They may look harmless—soft and fuzzy, even—but their tiny hairs can poke the skin and inject three chemicals: a histamine (irritates), acetylcholine (burns), and serotonin (causes pain). The result? A painful, acidic rash.

HOW TO: Treat a Nettle Rash

- Squirt the area with water, and wipe it off with the cleanest part of whatever you're wearing.

- Look for a nearby dock or jewelweed plant (see "Ahhh!," page 150), which often grow near stinging nettles. Tear off a leaf and rub the underside on the affected area. Or slice open the stem and rub it on the affected area.

- If no dock or jewelweed plant is in sight, make a mud paste (squirt water into dirt or spit into dirt) and apply it to the rash. When the mud dries, brush it off. (This removes the nettles.)

- Once home, clean the area with cold water and a clean towel or rag.

- Apply aloe vera, vinegar and water, or dish soap or hand soap and water, or make a paste of baking soda and water.

- When your skin is dry, apply adhesive tape to the area and remove the tape to try to extract nettles. Wipe with hydrogen peroxide when through.

OUCH! = American stinging nettle

2 to 5 feet tall; wiry green stem; soft-looking leaves; hollow, stinging hairs on stems and leaves ≣ Leaves 1 to 6 inches long with serrated edges ≣ Small brown or green flowers

OUCH! = Burning nettle

5 inches to 2 feet tall; stinging hairs on leaves and stems ≣ Smooth leaves give way to serrated leaves ≣ Flowers ≣ Small, triangular fruits

Ahhh! = Dock plant

2 to 5 feet tall; thick green-brown stem ≣ Green, fleshy leaves with small veins ≣ Small green or red flower clusters

Ahhh! = Jewelweed plant

2 to 6 feet tall; green stem; 1.5- to 3.5-inch leaves with scalloped margins and whitish underside ≣ Orange-and-red-speckled flower

Cactus

If you live and run in a dry environment, pay special attention to prickly succulents known as cacti. There are over 1,000 different types of cacti, and if you get any of their spiny needles stuck in your skin, you'll want to remove them immediately so they don't injure you further by poking deeper into your skin.

HOW TO: Remove Cactus Spines

- Use a stick to flick away larger cactus parts from your skin. (Do not use your fingers, as most cactus needles are covered with smaller needles.)

- Pull spines straight out. If possible, cover hands with material (ie: socks) to avoid smaller needles from lodging into your hands.

- Clean with water.

- Once home, use tweezers to remove any visible needles.

- Pour white school glue over the area. Let it dry. Peel it off. This will remove small, invisible needles. (Alternately, apply duct tape and peel it off, or rub a pumice stone or pantyhose back and forth to remove small needles.)

- Clean with antiseptic and cover with a bandage.

- If any part of a cactus remains in your skin, or if the area becomes red, inflamed, or pus-filled, seek medical help.

Cholla cactus (jumping cholla/teddy-bear cholla). These fuzzy cacti may look soft and cuddly, but their easily broken-off stems reach out and "hug" you, and their spines don't let go. The best way to remove a cholla ball is with a large plastic comb. If you don't have a comb, use a stick to remove the ball. Use tweezers or one of

the other methods described in "How to: Remove Cactus Spines,"
page 151, to remove any remaining tiny spines.

> ☀ If you're running in a cholla-rich environment, consider
> TIP carrying a comb.

Allergies

Some runners are more prone to seasonal allergies than others.
And the very nature of trails means major exposure to trees,
grasses, weeds, and molds.

HOW TO: Deal with Allergies

- Know what ails you, and choose trails wisely. If running
  along a trail lined with elm trees makes you feel horrible,
  then run along a different trail during the time of year when
  elm trees commonly release their pollen.

- Run at the end of the day. Most allergens are more active in
  the morning.

- Run after a rain or snowstorm. Falling moisture washes away
  many allergens. (If you're allergic to mold, however, know that
  moisture makes mold worse, and sunny days help dry it out.)

- Wash yourself and your clothes. Washing off pollens helps
  keep them from irritating your system.

- See a doctor. Allergists can advise on over-the-counter and
  prescribed allergy medications suitable for runners and can
  help you figure out what you're allergic to so you can adjust
  your running.

Environmental hazards

The weather can be formidable, but you don't necessarily have to be confined to treadmills because of clouds, a sweltering day, or a cold-snap storm that leaves behind a sheet of ice as your running surface. Mother Nature is your friend, albeit one to handle with respect and a high dose of smarts (and sometimes deference).

Lightning

There are clouds, and there are storm clouds. The darker the sky, the more likely that a thunderstorm is on its way. The safest way to avoid being struck by lightning is not getting caught in a storm in the first place. Listen to the forecast, check the area radar, and try to plan runs at times when storms are less likely.

Experts recommend waiting at least 30 minutes after any signs of **lightning and thunder** pass by to head outside.

If you do get caught out in a storm, run to a safe place as fast as you can. Safe places include inside a car or a building. Unsafe places include next to a tall or an isolated tree, under a shelter, or lying on the ground.

If reaching a safe place is not an option, seek a spot away from tall objects. Assume a crouching position, making your personal surface area as small as possible. Sit with your knees close together and your feet off the ground (on top of a pack or jacket, if possible.) This minimizes your surface area in an attempt to avoid ground currents.

Don't stand next to a tree or under a shelter. Side flashes jump from tall objects.

SAYS WHO

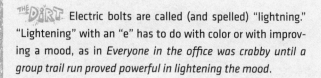

"If you're running with someone and get caught in a lightning storm, separate yourself from your running partner(s) at least 20 feet to minimize the potential of multiple casualties in the event of a direct strike."

LEO LLOYD, EMS training captain for Durango Fire and Rescue and medical rescue coordinator for the Hardrock 100-Mile Endurance Race

THE DIRT Electric bolts are called (and spelled) "lightning." "Lightening" with an "e" has to do with color or with improving a mood, as in *Everyone in the office was crabby until a group trail run proved powerful in lightening the mood.*

Only 3 to 5 percent of **lightning casualties** are due to a direct strike. The rest are from ground currents and side flashes. There are between 25 and 75 lightning-caused deaths per year in the United States.

Altitude illness

The most common form of altitude illness is acute mountain sickness (AMS). The more serious versions are high-altitude cerebral edema (HACE) and high-altitude pulmonary edema (HAPE). These ailments mostly afflict runners who travel from lower altitudes to higher altitudes to run.

Acute mountain sickness

AMS happens mostly at elevations above 8,000 feet but can affect people at lower elevations. Symptoms include headache, dizziness, nausea, vomiting, loss of appetite, weakness, difficulty sleeping, feeling chilled, and irritability. For runners who live at elevations below 3,000 feet and travel to a higher elevation, some precautions can help minimize the effects of altitude. For example, try to arrive at your higher-elevation running destination a few days early (at least).

Deal with it. Drink and eat more. Take a pain reliever to treat your headache. Do not continue to go higher. Descend to a lower elevation and continue to eat and drink.

THE DIRT. If your headache does not go away despite hydrating and taking a pain reliever, that's a good indication that you are suffering from AMS rather than simply dehydration or fatigue. Descend to a lower elevation.

High-altitude cerebral edema

HACE is a more severe form of altitude sickness that happens mostly over 13,000 feet and in conjunction with HAPE (see below). It's caused by the brain swelling with fluid, and symptoms include increased headache, lethargy, confusion, irritability, lack of coordination, vomiting, seizures, and the possibility of a coma and even death if not treated. Descend to a lower altitude immediately.

High-altitude pulmonary edema

HAPE is a very serious condition that happens when fluid accumulates in the lungs. Shortness of breath (even while sitting) and coughing (sometimes blood or frothy spit); bluish lips, skin, or fingernails; fast or shallow breathing; rapid heart rate; wheezing; and weakness or decrease in energy are all signs of HAPE—even if you have just one or two symptoms, you require immediate action. Treating HAPE requires descending to a lower elevation and often medical care, including oxygen.

Heat

Running in high temperatures poses a risk of not only dehydration but also heat exhaustion and heatstroke. For suggestions on what to wear when running in extreme heat, see "Weather the Weather," page 70.

Check the weather for the "apparent" heat. This is the combination of the temperature and humidity. Some weather web sites list dangerous conditions.

HEAT-RELATED PROBLEMS

	Symptom	Action
Hot	Feeling hot	Stay hydrated with electrolytes
Cramping	Cramping	Hydrate more with water and electrolytes Slow pace Massage cramp area
Heat exhaustion (debilitating)	Confusion, fatigue, dizziness, headache, cramping, nausea, pale skin, profuse sweating, elevated heart rate, dark urine	Hydrate with water and electrolytes Rest in shade Seek medical help Rest at least 24 hours
Heatstroke (potentially fatal)	High temperature, no sweating, fast heart rate, difficulty breathing, agitation, disorientation, hallucinations, seizure, coma	Seek medical help immediately Rest in shade Remove clothing to cool skin Apply ice to cool body (if no ice available, use water and fan to increase evaporative heat loss)

Frostbite

Frostbite isn't limited to mountaineers stranded on Mount Everest. When skin is exposed to the cold, either bare or under thin gloves or socks in freezing temperatures, runners can be at risk for one of four degrees of frostbite. While the differing degrees don't present themselves until the skin warms up (possibly days later), know that cold, white, waxy, numb skin suggests a cold injury.

What to do? Warm the skin in warm water or by putting bare skin next to bare skin (your own or your running partner's. It's a bonding experience). See a medical professional if your skin blisters or discolors in the days that follow exposure.

Snow blindness

Unprotected eyes can get fried on a clear day, but the harmful effects of the sun are exacerbated by reflective snow. The sun's rays reflect from snowy surfaces and bounce back up into your eyes—you're getting sun from both above and below you.

You won't feel the effects right away. But within hours, your eyes might feel gritty, as though you fell facefirst into a sandcastle.

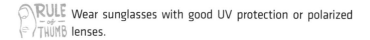 Wear sunglasses with good UV protection or polarized lenses.

 To **avoid frostbite**, check the weather (with the wind-chill factor), and dress appropriately, paying special attention to extremities such as feet, hands, and ears. (See "Weather the Weather," page 70.)

Ice

Icy surfaces are great for skating, not so great for running. If you find yourself on slick ground, shorten your stride and slow your pace. Seek out crunchy snow and widen your arm swing for additional balance. Wear shoes with toothy traction to stay surefooted. (See "Conditional Love," page 58.)

If you do fall on ice and hit your head, it's best to seek medical attention to rule out a concussion (See "Head Injury," page 135). And if bleeding persists anywhere on your body following a fall, seek medical attention. (See "Abrasions," page 133). You may need stitches.

Mystery aches and pains

Sometimes you ache, but you're not sure why—a painful Achilles, a sore knee, searing pain on the bottoms of your feet.

Perhaps it's an issue of overuse. Overuse injuries are muscles, other tissues, and bones that are overused either by doing too much too soon, not allowing your body to recover between workouts, or poor mechanics.

Many "mystery" injuries are caused by muscle imbalances, tightness, weakness, and overcompensation throughout our bodies. Use your body enough with any sort of imbalance, and an injury is sure to start hindering you.

To solve a mystery injury, consider seeing a medical professional who can assess your specific issues and provide a treatment plan for improvement. (See "Practitioners," page 162.)

 Activities that may help **prevent overuse injuries** include stretching, weight lifting, yoga, Pilates, and crosstraining.

Ice bath	Ice any and all parts to reduce swelling.	😟 💲
Massage	Massage sore, tight muscles.	😌 💵
Acupuncture	Stimulate acupuncture points with tiny needles.	😐 💵
Active release technique (ART)	Pressure-based elongation and/or mobilization of muscle and fascia.	😟 💵
Rolfing	Reorganize connective tissues; sort of like a massage on steroids. (Multiple sessions required)	😐 💵💵
Dry needling	Release trigger points with small needles (bigger than acupuncture needles).	😟 💵
Prolotherapy	Reinjure overstretched ligaments via injection to regenerate and tighten up said ligaments.	😐 💵💵
PRP	Promote healthy cells in injured area by extracting blood from healthy area, medically spinning it, and injecting good cells into injured area.	😐 💵💵

Key:

DRUG DEAL

Running and pain medications rarely mix. While pain meds may effectively ease pain or soreness, it is ill-advised to use them during exercise. For example, taking nonsteroidal anti-inflammatories (NSAIDs) such as ibuprofen while running can put you at risk for kidney damage, and acetaminophen can damage your liver. Talk to your doctor before taking any medication during a run. Read all labels and instructions on any over-the-counter pain medication before taking it.

Pain Meds	Nondrug Alternatives
Ibuprofen (e.g., Advil) is known to cause stomach distress, so take with food. (NSAID)	Arnica is an herb that is a natural anti-inflammatory and wound healer. It's mostly applied topically, but homeopathic remedies containing small amounts of arnica can be ingested.
Naproxen (e.g., Aleve) is a pain reliever and an NSAID.	Ice
Aspirin (e.g., Bayer) is a pain reliever and an NSAID.	Compression
Acetaminophen (e.g., Tylenol) is a pain reliever that is gentler on the stomach. It does not reduce swelling and is not an NSAID.	Beer

 Pain medications also **mask injuries**, meaning you could keep running when your body would otherwise tell you to stop.

Practitioners

- **Massage therapist.** Treats by massaging muscles using varying degrees of intensity.

- **Physical therapist.** Treats with manual therapy/massage, dry needling, ART, electric stimulation, ultrasound, or any combination of the above. Advises exercises for improvement and maintenance.

- **Chiropractor.** Adjusts bones and joints via manual and manipulative therapy.

- **Orthopedic doctor.** Assesses injury through examination and, sometimes, imaging (like X-rays or MRIs).

- **General practitioner.** Offers advice, gives referrals to physical therapists or orthopedic doctors, can order X-rays or MRIs.

- **Sports psychologist/psychologist.** Offers coping mechanisms for the emotional distress of being sidelined with an injury (and can also help with issues such as motivation, mental blocks to racing, etc.).

THE DEAL WITH STRETCHING

Some medical professionals believe in stretching; some do not. Some studies suggest that stretching is good for a runner; others suggest that stretching is bad for a runner. If stretching any or all muscles feels like a good idea for you, stretch after a run instead of beforehand. Or stretch partway through a run once muscles are warmer.

Self-care

A multitude of self-care tools on the market allows you to massage, stretch, brace, ice, heat, and palpate all of your own aching body parts. Owning one or more of these items lets you take matters into your own hands and can provide relief—or even prevent pain and problems in the first place.

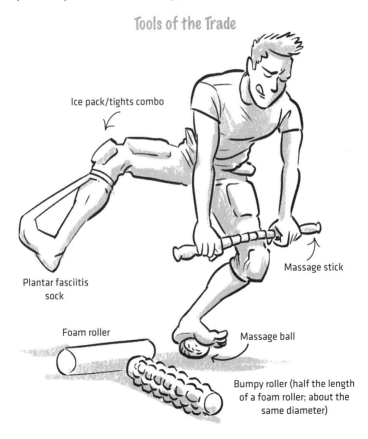

Tools of the Trade

Ice pack/tights combo

Massage stick

Plantar fasciitis sock

Foam roller

Massage ball

Bumpy roller (half the length of a foam roller; about the same diameter)

CHAPTER 9

Etiquette

etiquette \et-i-kit, -ket\ *n.* 1. The practices and forms prescribed by social convention or by authority. 2. A code of ethical behavior that makes the trail (and the world) a better place.

Etiquette isn't necessarily about hard-and-fast rules. It's mainly about good manners and courtesy. This chapter offers handy and important guidelines about everything from who has the right of way on a trail to how to best relieve yourself in the great outdoors to how to do our part to preserve nature.

Right of way

Runners aren't the only ones who use trails. Mountain bikers, equestrians, hikers, rock climbers, and birders are all trail users.

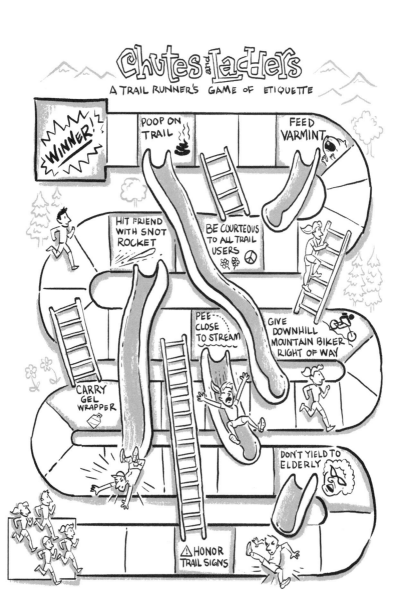

Some trails are wide enough for multiple trail users to pass one another, but others may be too narrow. Singletrack, by definition, is only wide enough for a single user, and so when two parties meet on a singletrack trail, one must yield to the other.

The International Mountain Bicycling Association created a trail courtesy sign, and it looks like this:

The basic principals are that bikes on the trail should yield to hikers, runners, and equestrians. Hikers and runners should yield to equestrians. Equestrians should keep an eye out for bikers, hikers, and runners and expect to have the right of way.

Are these guidelines always followed? No. Should trail users always pay attention to who's around them on the trail, be courteous to all, and pass and be passed nicely, regardless of "right of way"? Yes.

Considering that there are more than three user groups on trails, here's an updated trail courtesy sign to live by:

YIELD TO...

RULE of THUMB "Yield" means pull over to the side of the trail to let another pass. When yielding, it is polite to alert the other party that they've been yielded to and can proceed freely by saying something like *You're good*.

Two golden rules of the trail

- **Be courteous.** The most important thing for all trail users to remember is to be courteous. A smile and a friendly attitude go a long way in keeping everyone's trail experience positive.

- **Follow the rules.** In some instances, there are actual written rules. Some trail signs let users know who's allowed: horses, bikes, foot travelers, or some combination of these. Some signs alert users to one-way trails—most common at Nordic centers (open to runners in the dry months), and mountain bike centers. Some trails are open only to bikes on certain days of the week and only to foot travel and/or equestrians on other days. It is important for safety and courtesy to follow all trail signs.

Understanding the needs of others

Posted rule or not, putting yourself in the shoes of people you encounter on the trail and understanding their needs and their thinking can help you distinguish who should yield to whom.

Other trail runners. Encountering fellow trail runners while running can be a beautiful thing. You nod cheerfully to one another, say a simple *Hi*, and pass by knowing you're part of the same tribe.

Hikers. Trails are filled with hikers of many stripes. Casual hikers may be friends having a serious talk: *And then he said, "You're turning into your mother!" Oh, no, he didn't!* Or speed hikers wearing sweat-wicking performance apparel and a determined look on their faces. Or contemplative journalers: *I need to get to my rock.* And then there are families with small children, doing their best to share nature and keep meltdowns at bay.

These hikers are entitled to the trail as much as you are and aren't necessarily paying attention to you running, so let courtesy and common sense prevail.

Old couples holding hands. Older couples holding hands on trails should always have the right of way. Pass with care.

Up-to-somethings. Groups of young adults sometimes congregate on trails to smoke, drink, make out, or all of the above. Pass with care. And if you see your neighbor's kid, make a mental note as you pass by.

Dog walkers. Depending on the trail and the dog owner, canines may or may not be on a leash. Be friendly when you pass by, and consider lowering a hand for the dog to sniff. (For more on dogs, see "Dog," page 107.)

Birders/naturalists. Folks on the trail with binoculars, walking slowly while looking up, may be birders spotting warblers. Similar folks looking down may be naturalists hunting for mushrooms. Either will be busy identifying flora and fauna and may be unprepared to jump out of your way. Don't sneak up on them. Announce yourself with a friendly *hello*. (Or if you can screech like a low-swooping red-tailed hawk, try that.)

Equestrians. Horses are allowed on some of the same trails as runners. Take care not to spook a horse. Speak gently to it, and yield to the horse and rider, passing with care when there's room. Step to the downhill side of the trail or off to the side. Continue talking calmly as the animal passes by.

Mountain bikers. Mountain bikers sometimes get a bad rap for allegedly ripping around corners and charging down trails, scaring other trail users. But courteous mountain bikers don't cause problems; jerk mountain bikers (or runners or equestrians) do. While rules give foot traffic the right of way, let's face it: It's easier for you to move to the side of a trail than it is for them. Be courteous and consider giving them the right of way so they don't eat it.

Wheeled, motorized mechanisms. All-terrain vehicles, dirt bikes, and snowmobiles frequent certain trails. They're big, fast, and—thankfully—noisy, so you can get out of the way when you hear one. This is one of many good reasons to *not* wear headphones on a trail run.

 In some parts of the country, runners are banned from snowmobile trails during the winter months. Research rules in your area online.

Factors that influence who should yield to whom

Since right of way isn't always cut-and-dried, consider the following factors.

Momentum. Whoever relies on momentum and needs it to continue moving forward, and would have a hard time starting up again, should have the right of way. Examples include uphill mountain bikers, exhausted runners, and hikers doing all they can to keep one foot moving in front of the other.

Stopability. If a trail user would have a hard time stopping safely, consider yielding if only so he or she doesn't cream you on the trail and hurt both of you. Such users include runners sprinting down-

 Wearing headphones can compromise safety on the trail. All trail users benefit from one user being able to hear the other coming and acting accordingly.

hill with windmill arms, yelling *ahhhh!*; mountain bikers charging downhill fast; and older people or children hiking downhill.

Exertion level. If someone appears to be exerting him- or herself more than you—for example, you're on a casual run and they're doing speed work or running at tempo or huffing and puffing more than you—then the one exerting more effort should have the right of way. (Note that this doesn't necessarily mean the one who's going faster.)

Fear level. Take note of trail users who *jump* to the side of the trail. Be nice to them; they might be fragile. Horses might fall in this category, and so might other trail users in particular moods. Never sneak up on anyone. You may get a swift kick to the head, a frightened animal and rider, and an unsafe situation all around. (See "Equestrians," page 169.)

Jerkiness. Sometimes trail users, whether on foot, bike, or motorized vehicle, act like jerks. Despite guidelines, these folks will assume that they get the right of way and that what they're doing on the trail is more important than what you're doing. If you don't give them the right of way, they'll take it anyway. Don't let it ruin your day; step aside and take secret pleasure in knowing you are not a jerk.

 Don't be a jerk.

Safe passage

At some point you will pass—and be passed by—other trail users. Here's how to do it nicely.

HOW TO: Pass from Behind

- When approaching someone you want to pass, make a few subtle noises as you near them. For example, sniff or cough (or screech) a couple times. If this doesn't alert the person, or if the person doesn't give you room to pass, say *Hi there* or some other pleasantry.

- If they still don't move over so you can pass safely, say *Sorry, can I squeeze through?* or *On your left.* Don't forget to say *Thank you* as you pass by.

HOW TO: Pass Head-On

- Passing someone when you're facing each other is easier than passing from behind because you can see each other coming. Edge to the side of the trail, continuing to run as you make room for him or her to get by.

Do not yell *On your left!* with no other warning of your presence. This tends to agitate trail users. To see how to say this in other languages, see "Destination Races," page 239.

- If the trail is narrow—or if it's an equestrian, a pack of bikers, or a motorized vehicle—move completely off the trail until the other party passes by.

HOW TO: Be Passed

- If you hear someone coming up behind you who you suspect wants to pass, look back to see how far away that person is and move to the side as you continue running. If the trail is narrow, consider hopping off trail for a moment so they can pass. If the passer tucks in behind you instead of passing, say something like *Let me know if you want to get by me.*

- When being passed, smile and be pleasant to show you are A-OK with the fact that someone faster just passed you (even if your ego is bruised).

RULE of THUMB If you're running side by side with a friend as another trail user approaches, move to single-file formation so the other person can pass by.

 When **passing an equestrian**, talk calmly and pass on the lower side of the trail, if there is one.

Eliminating

Everybody pees and poops. And most people blow boogers out their noses and loogies out their mouths, too. Some people need to do one or all of the above during a trail run.

Unlike on road runs, there are no toilets available in the woods (aside from, maybe, an outhouse in a park). There are also no coffee shops or neighbors' houses where one can duck in for a civilized place to eliminate.

So where—and how—should a trail runner take care of business in the woods?

Peeing

If you're hydrating properly, you may well have to urinate during your runs. If you don't feel that urge, you're likely either on a short run or you should be drinking more.

What's the etiquette for peeing on the trail? A few factors weigh in here.

How far off the trail? Getting out of sight and sound to minimize social impact is recommended. And when you step off trail, seek out durable ground: rock, gravel, sand, dry grass, decomposing forest floor (bark or fallen leaves). Avoid fragile flora such as moss, broadleaf plants, or flowers.

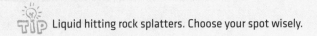 Liquid hitting rock splatters. Choose your spot wisely.

How far from water? To keep streams and lakes clean and safe for animals as well as trail users who might be filtering water to drink, aim to relieve yourself a good distance from any water source.

How hidden? In forested areas, a nearby tree should do the trick. But on some trails, there's nowhere to hide, no matter how far you go off the trail. How hidden should you be? That depends. If the trail is empty, move off and away from the trail but don't bother hiding. If the trail is busy or you are with another runner, move farther off the trail to find a concealed spot.

Relieving yourself on a group run

Relieving yourself in a group situation can be tricky. But keep in mind, everybody has business and needs to take care of it. Plus, you're all runners—which is to say, you're practically family.

To handle the situation with grace, drop off the pace and say *I'll catch up*, with no further information. Do your business, and catch up to the group. (They may slow their pace a bit to let you catch up.)

Mechanically speaking

Since men and women come with different parts, the mechanics of peeing in the great outdoors are also different.

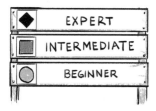

Men. Given their anatomy, men have an easier time peeing quickly and discreetly.

Pull shorts down just enough while standing.	⬤
Pee out the bottom/side of shorts while standing.	◼
Kneel on one knee and pee out the bottom/side of shorts.	◆

Women. Women have more work to do when it comes to peeing quickly and discreetly.

Squat with shorts down.	⬤
Squat or kneel on one knee. Pull bottom of shorts to the side and pee.	◼
Bend over with hands on knees and shorts down.	◆

Whichever method you choose, make sure all material—shorts, tights, liner—is *out of the path of danger*.

Pooping

Some folks rarely have to poop while on a trail run. For others, the need is unfortunately frequent.

How far off the trail and away from water? Try to step on rocks, dry grasses, or gravel instead of broadleaf plants, moss, or flowers. A

 A method favored by ultrarunners **too tired to squat** all the way down or afraid they won't be able to get all the way back up.

safe distance is considered at least 200 feet[*][*] off trail and away from any drainages or running or still water.

How hidden? Very hidden. Nobody wants to see anybody else pooping. Ever.

Mechanically speaking

Whether male or female, pooping in the woods requires squatting. Either lower your drawers  or use the pull-to-the-side method ◆ (this should be attempted only if you are wearing loose shorts or a skirt with a brief-style liner).

⚠ WARNING

Whichever method you choose, ensure that all material—shorts, tights, liner—is *out of the path of danger.*

HOW TO: Poop in the Woods

- Go at least 200 feet away from the trail.
- Grab a stick or pointy rock and dig a hole 6 to 8 inches deep.
- Do your thing.
- If you have toilet paper or wipes and a well-sealing plastic bag, wipe and take the paper with you. 🐦

Two hundred feet is the distance recommended by the Leave No Trace Center for Outdoor Ethics, a nonprofit organization whose mission is to teach people to enjoy the outdoors responsibly.

If you don't have **toilet paper** or wipes, use a broad, smooth, nontoxic leaf or flat rock. (See "Plant-Inflicted Hazards," page 146.) Snow works, too.

- Bury whatever came out of you. And bury it well.

- Return to the trail by stepping on rocks, gravel, or dry grasses instead of flowers, broadleaf plants, or moss.

Other bodily fluids and functions

Pee and poop aren't the only things that come out of a trail runner's body.

Runny nose

Sometimes exertion causes a runny nose. Or maybe you have sinus issues that keep you sniffing and snorting while you run. Or maybe you've got a cold.

Try a powerful sniff. Or use your sleeve, shirt, or a glove to wipe viscous dripping fluids. If all else fails, employ the all-powerful snot rocket.

HOW TO: Blow a Snot Rocket

- Make sure no trail users are within 10 feet[*] of the area in which you aim to blow.

- Slow or stop[**] as you turn your head to the side of the clogged nostril.

---

[*] Fifteen feet if you have a particularly **hearty blow**.

[**] **With practice**, you'll be able to do this without slowing your stride.

- Close off the air to the other nostril with your index finger.
- Blow hard and away from your body.
- Repeat on the other side if needed.

Spit

Some runners drum up excess saliva while they run. This may be due to allergies (increased reactions to pollen while running creates more postnasal drip), cold air (your body produces mucus as a humidifier), or exertion (bodies produce saliva at varying levels when challenging lungs and cardiovascular systems).

Before spitting, ensure that no trail users are within spitting distance of the area in which you aim to spit. Spit hard and away from your body, preferably off to the side of the trail.

Burps

Burps are not uncommon when you run. Some runners even burp excessively, perhaps due to the jostling. If you're in the latter group, consider changing your mode of hydration (swallowing too much air can increase burping) or experimenting with your diet to see if that decreases your burping. But generally speaking, burping on the run is fine and can make you feel better. Just say *Excuse me.*

No one wants to see a **globule of spit** in the middle of the trail where they're placing their feet.

Passing gas

As with burping, some folks pass gas a lot when they run. Exercise helps decrease bloating, which your body deals with by expelling gas. The jostling of each running step is an instigator as well.

If you're running alone and there's no one around, you're good. If you're running in company, you have options. You can acknowledge the sound but tell people nearby that it was your shoe. Or a frog. Or you can cough or make some other attempt to mask the sound[a] that just came out of you. Or you can just own it and say *Excuse me*.

If you'd like to experience *less* gas while you run, consider a change in your diet, especially prerun. Certain foods that may cause excessive gas include bran, beans, too much fruit, cabbage-family vegetables, too many starches, dairy, oatmeal, and soda.

RULE of THUMB If you're running in a group and feel gas coming on, drop to the back of the pack. There is no need to explain yourself. Your move will be greatly appreciated even if they never know why you dropped back.

Vomit

Vomiting on the trail is hopefully limited to unlucky ultrarunners during a race and pregnant runners in their first trimester. The rule is simple: If you suddenly need to expel bile, do your very best to aim off trail.

 If there was **no sound**, anyone behind you is likely in trouble. Be prepared for hazing.

Sweat

Runners sweat. Some profusely. Don't be ashamed. You're engaging in a sport, and sports make you sweat.🐾 But consider fist-bumping fellow trail runners after a great run rather than giving them a big, wet bear hug.

Preserving the trail

Trails are gifts that keep on giving. By making preservation efforts, we ensure that our grandchildren's grandchildren can enjoy wonderful trail running adventures, too.

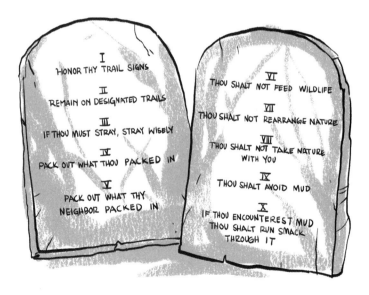

I
HONOR THY TRAIL SIGNS

II
REMAIN ON DESIGNATED TRAILS

III
IF THOU MUST STRAY, STRAY WISELY

IV
PACK OUT WHAT THOU PACKED IN

V
PACK OUT WHAT THY NEIGHBOR PACKED IN

VI
THOU SHALT NOT FEED WILDLIFE

VII
THOU SHALT NOT REARRANGE NATURE

VIII
THOU SHALT NOT TAKE NATURE WITH YOU

IX
THOU SHALT AVOID MUD

X
IF THOU ENCOUNTEREST MUD THOU SHALT RUN SMACK THROUGH IT

🐾 To make yourself more comfortable, try a headband, a hat, or a visor with a sweat-wicking band and apparel that **wicks away sweat** and simultaneously fights odor.

I. Honor thy trail signs. Trail signs are posted for a reason (or three), and those reasons involve preserving the trail, preserving the natural habitat of the trail, or keeping the peace among trail users.

Honor and obey these signs. Ignoring them not only puts the peace at risk but also puts the trail at risk for being closed to runners and other users. Land managers don't like it when their signs are ignored.

II. Thou shalt remain on designated trails. Unless you need to leave the trail to do some business (and even then, see Commandment III), you should stay on designated trails. Occasionally you may be tempted to bushwhack off trail to check out a view, take a shortcut, or look for wild raspberries. Keep in mind that doing so puts the natural habitat at risk (and that plants often whack back).

Remaining on the trail also means not cutting corners—don't beeline straight up or down a hillside instead of following the switchbacks. Doing so can damage the area.

III. If thou must stray, stray wisely. If you do bushwhack, travel on the hardest, most durable ground you can find— rocks, logs, woody plants, or dry grasses. Avoid stepping on fragile flora such as moss, lichen, and alpine plants. These plants take an exceptionally long time to recover.

If you bushwhack in a group, don't run single file. Spread out to minimize repeated footsteps over a single area. And choose a different route on your way back to the trail—doing so will minimize impact.

IV. Thou shalt pack out what thou hast packed in. Also known as *Pack it in; pack it out*, this principle means *Don't litter on the trail.* Do your due diligence in not leaving behind the tops of gel packets, corners of energy-bar wrappers, or toilet paper. Other trail users deserve a trash-free nature experience, and garbage left on the trail can harm wildlife.

V. Thou shalt pack out what thy neighbor hast packed in. This is more than just a good deed. By shoving a wayward gel wrapper in your pack, you're bettering your environment and that of everyone around you.

VI. Thou shalt not feed wildlife. You are not doing that cute chipmunk, emaciated deer, or chirping marmot any favors by sharing your food. Feeding human treats to wildlife endangers them in more ways than one: Your food could make them sick or change their behavior.

Say you feed a chipmunk. Word spreads among his friends that there are energy bars down by the trail. Many chipmunks start coming near the trail. The chipmunks start fighting for energy bars, injuring each other. Or a coyote gets word of the party and comes down to prey on the chipmunks.

The human-animal feeding relationship lessens an animal's natural fear of people, a fear that is necessary for both animal and human safety. Animals can become more aggressive toward humans when they learn to expect handouts.

Finally, feeding animals brings a higher concentration of animals to a particular area, which can help spread diseases among them.

VII. Thou shalt not rearrange nature. Although a downed log or a slew of babyhead rocks may be a nuisance to navigate around, leave them be. The trails are likely the way they are for reasons of sustainability: minimizing erosion and encouraging healthy water drainage. Plus, other trail users, such as mountain bikers, are sometimes attached to natural features even if they seem like obstacles.

ba·by·head rock \ˈbā-bē-hed ˈräk\ *n. (pl. –s)* 1. Smooth, roundish rock shaped and sized like a baby's head.

VIII. Thou shalt not take nature with you. It is very tempting to pick a bouquet of wildflowers; grab a giant, heart-shaped boulder; or bring home a stick shaped like a light saber for your kid, but refrain. Leave nature behind for everyone to enjoy in his or her own way.

IX. Thou shalt avoid mud. Avoid muddy trails. Running on muddy trails damages the trail, with your footprints splattering the surface at every step. On a rainy day (or season), that means either finding a well-draining trail, sticking to the roads (or treadmill) for your run, or seeking out a dry trail.

Fellow trail runners in your area can help you figure out which local trails have the best drainage and therefore are the least muddy. Try calling a running or an outdoor store for tips and insider information.

X. If thou encounterest mud, thou shalt run smack through it. Should you encounter a muddy section of a trail, either turn around and go another way or run through the middle of the trail. Stepping off to the side widens the trail and causes more damage to the habitat than does traipsing right down the middle.

CHAPTER 10

Company: Running with Human or Animal Friends

Running alone can be just what the doctor ordered (See "Your Mind," page 16). But running in the company of friends—old, new, human, canine, or equine—can offer rewards that running alone cannot.

Running solo

There is a lot to be said for running by yourself. You can run at your own pace without feeling that you should speed up or slow down to match someone else. You can head out on a whim, whenever you feel like running or have a window of time, without having to coordinate with anyone else's schedule. You can hear the rhythm of your own breath and feet against the earth. And you have your thoughts to yourself. Some of the world's great problems—or at least many of our own smaller ones—have been solved on a solo trail run.

Benefits of running alone:
- Enjoy peace and quiet
- Be alone with your thoughts
- Run at your own pace
- Go at a moment's notice
- Extend or shorten your run as you please
- Enjoy nature with no distractions

Staying safe

The joys of running solo are many, but there are a few safety precautions to consider.

Tell someone where you're going. Even if you're just going for a short out-and-back on a neighborhood trail, it's a good idea to let someone know where you're headed and roughly when you'll be back.

Don't wear headphones. Wearing headphones and listening to music or books on tape makes you less alert to your surroundings—bikes or runners coming up behind you, animals rustling in the bushes, etc. Having all senses on the alert adds safety. If you must listen to something, wear one earbud in and one out, and keep the volume low.

Know where you're going. Getting a little lost on a trail run can make for an adventure and a good story. Getting a lot lost on a trail run, however, can turn into an ordeal you didn't bargain for, particularly when you are alone. Do your homework if you're trying a new trail. (See "Staying Found," page 30.)

Bring a phone. Consider carrying a phone when running alone so that if you twist an ankle, get lost, or bonk, you can call someone to let them know you'll be a while—or that you need help. A phone with GPS can be particularly handy (see "Staying Found," page 30).

Running in company

Many of us find community on the trail with other runners. The shared experience of running amidst nature, like kids playing in the woods, can turn individuals into a tribe. And running buddies can be as tight as family.

Sometimes you might run with a friend or two, and sometimes you might feel like expanding your circle and joining up with a local running group.

Benefits of running with a friend:
- Spend quality time together
- Catch up on gossip or trade training tips
- Motivate each other to go running
- Motivate each other to run farther or faster
- Keep each other honest
- Keep each other safe

Be good company

Everyone wants to run with people whose company they enjoy. Here are a few reminders about how to be a desirable running companion.

Be on time. Your friend is waiting for you; respect that. If you're running late, a call or a text goes a long way.

Don't wear headphones. It's not much fun to run with someone who's more interested in their music than in their running companion.

Be positive. It's fine to exclaim the occasional *This hill's a beast!*, as there can be solidarity in that. But constant complaining—*This run is too hard!* or *It's cold!* or *You're so much faster than me!*—is a downer.

Don't let your ego run. Refrain from saying things like *I'm tired from being third in my age group yesterday, so this pace is fine.*

Be flexible, to a point. If your friend wants to run a little longer, shorter, faster, slower, or in a different direction, be flexible. But if your friend wants to add another 14,000-foot peak, it's reasonable to part ways and complete your planned run on your own.

Running with friends of different speeds

Have an idea of how speedy (or not) your friends are, and plan your runs accordingly. If you're in training to PR at an upcoming trail half-marathon and your friend is a casual jogger, plan to run with that friend on your slower or recovery days and go at whatever speed he or she wants. On the other hand, if you know your friend is faster than you or likes to run longer or on more challenging terrain, plan on running with that friend on your harder days and know what you're in for.

If you want to slow down a faster friend, try this. At the base of a big climb, ask an open-ended question:

What do you think about the president?

Do you believe in God?

How's it going with _____? (Fill in the blank with the name of your fast friend's significant other, parent, child's teacher, etc.)

Your friend will start talking, and keep talking, which takes up oxygen and forces him or her to slow down a little.

If, on the other hand, you want to speed up a slower friend, *do not* ask an open-ended question while running. Let your friend set the pace as well as the tone of the conversation, and plan to save your harder efforts (and inquisitions) for another day.

Benefits of running with running groups:
- Make new friends and running partners
- Have motivation to go running
- Discover new trails
- Share the beauty of the trail with others
- Learn from more experienced runners
- Run farther or faster (or slower or shorter) than you normally would
- Stay safe

Joining a running group

Running stores and running clubs often host social group runs one or more times a week. Ask an employee at a running store, or look online for area trail running clubs.

Generally speaking, all speeds and abilities are welcome at group trail runs. The exceptions are trail running teams and competitive clubs that meet for group workouts to push each other and commiserate in the joyful pain of speed workouts and hill repeats.

Be a good group member

The group is probably never going to disinvite you, but you don't want them wishing they could.

Be on time. The run leader won't want everyone else who showed up on time to wait around for very long. Plus, the run leader won't necessarily know you're coming, which means you may inadvertently get left behind. Group runs tend to head out within 5 or 10 minutes of the appointed meeting time.

Don't wear headphones. Not being able to hear or talk to others on a group run makes you antisocial, which mostly defeats the purpose of a group run.

Be flexible, to a point. If the group takes a trail you've never run before because you've been intimidated, go with it. Trying new trails, distances, or speeds in a group allows you to see what you can do with the support of others around you. Who knows? You may find your new favorite trail. But if the group decides to climb a mountain and you're nursing an injury, by all means take care of yourself and do only what feels right.

Avoid showing off. Group dynamics bring out a competitive spirit in some people. If you're feeling fit and fast, you may be tempted to run ahead or brag about your accomplishments. Know that most people don't love it when others do this.

Don't drop people. Wherever you are in the pack, be aware of the speeds of those behind you, and never turn at a trail junction without the runners behind you seeing which way you went. (Most groups will wait for all members at trail junctions before heading in a new direction.) Help the leader by doing your part to ensure that no one gets dropped from a run. Being dropped could leave a runner lost, as group runs often take new routes linking multiple trails.

Exit gracefully. If you decide to bail from a run for any reason, tell someone, ideally the group leader. If you disappear silently from the group, you'll send a wave of worry and maybe even a search party out after you.

Don't hit on other runners. Or, if you do find a fellow group member particularly intriguing, get a little intel before making a move.

intel \in-'tel\ n. 1. Insider knowledge, such as marital status, gained by asking questions like *What are your plans for the holidays?*

Running with dogs

If you run with a dog, you already know the rewards. If you never have, you should experience it at least once. Consider borrowing a dog from a friend.

Benefits of running with dogs:
- Added safety
- A running partner who goes where, when, and at what pace you want

Qualities in a dog that may impair your pace: old, tired, too small, not a breed that likes to run. (See "Special Canine Considerations," page 196.)

- Motivation to get out and run . . . dogs need exercise
- A joyful companion
- Dog smiles rub off on humans

Know the rules

It's important to know the dog-related rules on the trails where you plan to run. Some trails allow dogs on leash. Some allow dogs that are voice-controlled and not on a leash, and a voice-controlled dog might have to wear a colored tag on its collar that proves that the owner went through the proper voice-control procedures for your area. Some trails, such as those in many national parks, don't allow dogs.

What to bring when running with a dog

A leash. Whether the trail allows dogs off leash or not, it's advisable to have a leash with you. There may be times when you need to put the dog on a leash, if only for a short while—for example, you need to keep your dog from chasing a pack of deer; someone on the trail near you is afraid of dogs; you don't want your dog jumping in a pond of stagnant water.

A poop bag. It's simple common courtesy—and sometimes the law—to pick up after your dog and dispose of the poop. It is also a health issue, as poop spreads disease and contaminates water. Always have a poop bag on you.

If your dog **pulls excessively** on the leash when you run together, consider using a harness to minimize tracheal irritation—hers from pulling while wearing a regular collar and yours from yelling.

Tying a **plastic bag** around your leash ensures that you always have a bag on you. Plus, it's more comfortable than running with a bag in your pocket or in your hand.

Extra water. If you run with a water bottle or hydration bladder, teach your dog to lick the stream of water like it's coming out of a hose, and bring extra water for your dog to drink. If your dog won't drink this way, carry a collapsible fabric bowl or try squirting water into your cupped hand for him to drink.

A towel. Trails can be muddy and dusty, and they often have creeks or ponds nearby that are irresistible to your dog. Having a towel in your car allows you to wipe down your dog or cover your seats to protect your car from grime.

IS THERE A POOP FAIRY?

When a dog owner has a bag, scoops up his or her dog's poop, and leaves the full bag on the side of the trail, he or she is *probably* planning to pick up the bag on the way back to the trailhead (rather than run the entire trail carrying a bag of poop). When dog owners do not pick up the bags they left, for whatever reason, it's possible that they believe a magical poop fairy will flutter by to pick it up.

There is no such thing as a poop fairy.
Pick up your dog's poop, and dispose of the poop bags.

Special canine considerations

Know your dog. Even if you have great faith in your dog's ability to run long distances at high speeds, err on the side of caution. The dog's health depends on you not running him too much, too fast. Dogs will rarely let you know that they're too tired. They want to keep going with you, and they will try even if it's too much for them. Talk to your veterinarian about what is appropriate for your dog's breed, age, and personality.

Know the trails. Choosing trails wisely can make a difference in both your and your dog's experience. Running technical or hilly trails slows *you* down, which is a good thing for your pup because it makes the pace more manageable.

Watch the heat. Heat exhaustion and heatstroke affect dogs more than humans. While humans sweat to regulate their body temperatures, dogs do not. Dogs pant to cool off but can suffer from problems caused by heat. In hot weather, plan to run near a creek or other natural water source so your pup can cool off, and seek out trails with a lot of shade.

Know the flora. Certain parts of the natural world should be avoided when running on a trail with your dog. Oils from poison oak, poison ivy, and sumac can get on your dog's fur and then be spread throughout your home and among your family. If you know your dog ran through any of these plants, wash her with an oil-removing soap, as you would yourself. (See "Plant-Inflicted Hazards," page 146.)

Respect the fauna. Keep your dog from terrorizing wild animals—except possibly squirrels who may have eaten the tomatoes out of your garden.

Watch out for ride-alongs. Running in the wild with your dog exposes her to prickers, burrs, and ticks. Check your dog's fur after running in areas rife with any of the above, and remove any you find. (For more on tick removal, see "Ticks," page 142.)

Prepare for cold and snow. If you run on a snowy trail and your dog starts limping or whining, check his paws for ice balls. Remove ice balls promptly. In bad weather, consider covering the dog's paws with booties, which may be found at pet stores or online. (Know that some dogs will refuse to wear booties, gnawing at them and shaking them off until you resign yourself to losing the money you spent.)

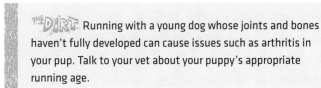

THE DIRT Running with a young dog whose joints and bones haven't fully developed can cause issues such as arthritis in your pup. Talk to your vet about your puppy's appropriate running age.

Running with horses or burros

While canine companions are the most popular running buddies, they are not the only possibility for nonhuman company on the trail. If you enjoy large hairy or furry mammals, there are a few more options.

 "Burro" is the Spanish word for "donkey."

Benefits of running with animals of the equine sort:

- A running partner who can carry your gear
- Motivation to get out and run . . . horses and burros need exercise
- A joyful companion
- A new appreciation for animals
- A fun way to invigorate your running with a new experience

Logistics

Running with a horse or burro isn't limited to those who own horses or burros. Some folks who raise said animals are happy to lend them out for trail runs. Many of these setups revolve around either Ride and Tie events (horse and two runners; see page 199) or burro races (burro and runner; see page 200).

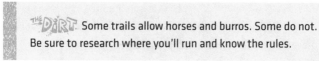

THE DIRT Some trails allow horses and burros. Some do not. Be sure to research where you'll run and know the rules.

What to bring when running with a horse or burro

A roll-with-it attitude. Running with a horse or burro sets you up for a great life lesson: When things seem somewhat out of your control, just keep moving.

A sense of humor. Animals can be funny, and if you stop long enough to realize that you're out running on trail with a horse or burro as a buddy, appreciate the humor in it.

A lot of patience. Trying to get an animal that weighs hundreds of pounds to do something that they might not be in the mood for can be trying for both parties. Have patience.

Empathy for your animal. Especially when racing in an equine/ human event, respect and appreciate your animal partner.

A lot of water. Ensure that a horse or burro is well fed and watered before a run or an event. They can store water like camels. You, on the other hand, cannot. Running with a horse or burro is a lot of work, physically and mentally, and you'll want to remember to drink. Bring enough.

Ride and Tie racing tips

Ride and Tie events involve two runners and a horse as a team of three. One team member starts the race running, while the other rides the horse or leads it by the reins. The first rider rides as far as he or she thinks the runner can run at a decent pace, then dismounts and ties the horse to a fence post or tree and takes off running. The first runner gets to the horse, mounts it or leads it by the reins, and continues before trading off again, and so on. Races are between 20 and 100 miles.

Wear trail running gear. Despite your time in the saddle, you'll still be running. Dress appropriately for running; think wicking apparel and trail running shoes more than flannel, chaps, and boots.

Add long socks and a helmet. You'll want protection for your lower legs, and you're required to wear a helmet. Running in a helmet saves time in transitioning between riding and running.

Find a good team. A good team is a solid, experienced horse and a solid, experienced human—both of whom you get along with and with whom you share common goals.

Be a good teammate. Get to know your horse and your human. Train together. Be flexible and supportive, all the things you want a good partner to be.

Train your core. Don't underestimate the toll that mounting and dismounting a horse will take on your body. Train your core to prepare yourself. (See "Getting Stronger and Faster," page 202.)

Strategize. Planning who runs first, who rides when, and so on can make a big difference in placing and in your overall race experience.

Hydrate and fuel. There will be vet checks for your horse but not for you. Take care of yourself as you would in a human-only race. (See "Nutrition," page 82.)

Burro racing tips

Burro racing involves events in which a runner leads a burro (or the burro leads the runner) through a trail race. These races take place in mountain towns of Colorado. Runners are not allowed to ride the burros, and the burros must, symbolically, carry what miners carried in the mid-1800s: saddlebags and a pick, a gold pan, and a shovel. This kit must weigh at least 33 pounds. Races are between 4 and 29 miles long.

Wear trail running gear. You may be out on a trail with a burro, but you're still on a trail run. Wear shoes with traction and other accoutrements to keep you comfortable.

Consider gloves. You'll be leading or being led by your burro with a rope. Thick gloves can save your hands from blisters (but can also hinder your control of the rope).

Drink. It's easy to get caught up in all the wrangling and coercing, otherwise known as running in harmony with your donkey. Be sure to stay hydrated, especially since burro races take place in the Colorado high country, which has particularly thin and dry air.

Drink wisely. You'll want your hands free, so wear a hydration pack with an easily accessible hydration hose. Crafty burro racers rig up hydration systems on the saddlebags and drink from them when they need to, thus allowing the weight to be carried by the stronger animal.

Be good to your burro. Your burro is your teammate. Treat your donkey as you'd like to be treated: with patience, respect, and encouragement.

Embrace the challenge. A burro race is a wild adventure. Enjoy it!

THE DIRT Mules, which are part horse, are not allowed in burro races.

For more on all types of events, see "Trail Racing," page 232.

CHAPTER 11

How, Part II: Getting Stronger and Faster

Being a trail runner means finding a natural surface somewhere and simply running. Anyone can do it. But maybe you want to see what your body can do, either in a race or with your own personal, nonracing goals. Good news! There are ways to get stronger and faster, go farther, and become generally more badass.

Home improvement

Exercises you can do at home or in a gym can help prevent injury and make your body stronger, which in turn makes you both faster and more durable.

STRONGER Feet and Ankles

WHY. Feet and ankles act as a solid base and do an enormous amount of work with every step, controlling the upward forces

through your legs and hips and into your spine. (For another ankle exercise, see "An Ounce of Prevention," page 131.)

(For another ankle exercise, see "An Ounce of Prevention," page 131.)

Standing arch lift

- Stand with your bare feet flat on the floor, *pronating* so your midfoot/arch sags toward the ground.

- Engage the muscles in your foot and lower leg to raise your arch while not allowing your big toe to lift off the floor.

- Do this with both feet at once, holding the position in a controlled manner until fatigue makes you lose form.

- Advance to balancing on one leg at a time in this position, holding until fatigued.

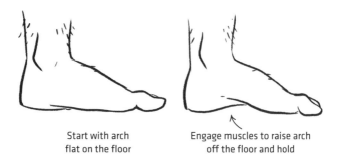

Start with arch   Engage muscles to raise arch
flat on the floor   off the floor and hold

pronating \ˈprō-nā-tiŋ\ *v.* 1. Inward and downward rotation of the bones and tissues in the midfoot that causes the foot's arch to sag inward and downward toward the ground when walking or running. 2. Potential cause of a whole host of running injuries if not addressed.

When doing exercises, it is okay to become tired and shaky. But when you become so fatigued that you begin losing proper form, it's time to stop and rest. Quality is more important than quantity.

Ankle-band series

- Wrap a band around a fixed point (e.g., a bedpost), and sit on the floor with your right leg straight and your left leg bent with the bottom of your left foot flat on the floor. Loop the other end of the band over the top of your right midfoot so there's tension in the band, and place your hands flat on the floor for support.

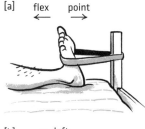

[a] flex ← point →

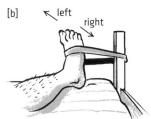

[b] ← left right ↘

- Flex [a] and point your right foot through the full range of motion, 8 to 10 times.

- Turn your body 90 degrees so the band wraps around the upper inside of your foot. Stabilize your lower leg with your left leg and foot to keep the working leg still. Pull [b] and release the band from side to side through the full range of motion, 8 to 10 times.

- Reposition your body, this time turning in the opposite direction (180 degrees) from the last position so that the band is wrapped around the upper outside of your right foot. Cross your left leg over your right leg and stabilize the working leg with your left foot. Pull and release the band from side to side though the full range of motion, 8 to 10 times. Aim for smooth, full range of movement in each position.

- Switch legs and repeat the series.

STRONGER Lower Legs, Core, and Glutes

WHY. Strengthening leg muscles and tissues around knee and hip joints with controlled, dynamic movements integrates the psoas and other core muscles so they work together with your legs when you're out on the trail.

HOW
Hamstring curls on a Swiss ball

- Lie on your back with your heels up on the ball and arms out to the sides, palms down.

- Raise your torso to a bridge position.

- Activate your glutes and bend your knees to roll the ball toward your butt, raising hips higher as you do so. (You'll be rolling the ball from your heels to the soles of your feet.)

- Roll the ball back out to starting position.

- Continue until fatigued.

- When you can do 3 sets of 12 to 15 double-leg curls, try single-leg curls.

Single-leg split squats
- Standing in a split-legged position, with your hands on your hips and your upper body upright, place the top of your back foot on a chair or bench behind you.

- Shift your weight to the front heel and drive your front knee forward and outward so your knee tracks over your foot.

- Lower your body toward the floor, stopping when the thigh of your front leg is parallel to the floor. Your front knee should not extend past your front foot.

- Do as many repetitions as you can on the same leg to fatigue. (If you focus on keeping your weight in your heel, you should feel this in your butt and hip more than in your quadriceps.) Return to starting position, and switch legs.

- When you can maintain good form doing 15 repetitions per leg, add hand weights, holding them with straight arms by your sides.

STRONGER Gluteus Medius and Core

WHY. Your gluteus medius keeps your hip rotator cuff functioning properly and helps keep your core and your legs working together effectively, especially through side-to-side movements and climbing/descending. These muscles are responsible for how the knees behave and for protecting them from injury.

Clamshell progression

• Lie on your side with your legs stacked on top of each other and slightly bent. Activate your core.

• Keeping heels together, slowly raise [a] and lower the knee of your top leg 5 times.

• Keeping your knees together, raise and lower the foot [b] of your top leg 5 times.

• Lift your top leg so it hovers a few inches above your lower leg. Raise [c] and lower the knee of your upper leg 5 times, keeping heels roughly 2 inches apart.

• Raise and lower the foot of your upper leg [d] 5 times, keeping your knees roughly 2 inches apart.

• Extend your hip behind the midline of your body, keeping abs tight and the thigh of your upper leg still. Raise and lower your lower leg [e] 5 times.

• Repeat this series 3 to 5 times without rest between sets. Aim for a full range of movement and smooth control.

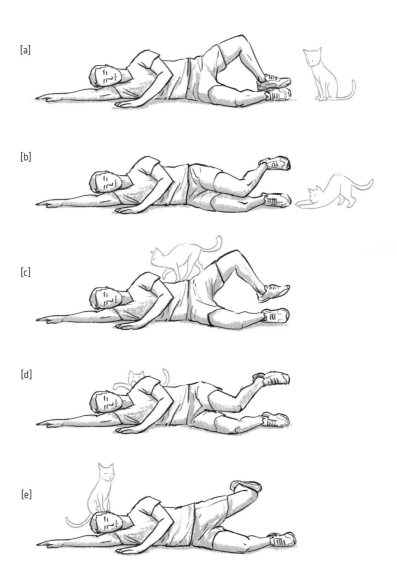

[a]

[b]

[c]

[d]

[e]

[a] [b]

Monster walks

- Place a band around your ankles, bend your knees slightly, and place your hands on your hips or waist [a].

- Keeping your upper body upright and still, step sideways with your left foot [b] to tighten the tension on the band, and follow with the right foot. Do this until fatigued.

- Stepping sideways, return the way you came.

- Step out diagonally with your right foot to tighten the tension on the band, then step with the left foot. Do this until fatigued.

- Step backward diagonally the way you came. Repeat in the other direction.

- Step forward as if walking a tightrope, swinging your front leg around in a wide arc and placing it in line with your back foot. Do this until fatigued.

- Return backward the way you came.

STRONGER Upper Body and Core

WHY. Core and upper-body strength help you maintain balance and power uphill and help keep you steady downhill and over technical terrain. An effective arm swing and trunk rotation facilitate faster leg turnover and more powerful strides.

HOW
Push-ups
- With your toes or knees on the ground, place your hands flat on the ground directly under your shoulders.

- Activate your core and shoulder blades to remain in a straight plank position.

- Slowly lower to the ground by bending your elbows, making sure your elbows don't flare out too far from your sides, stopping just before your nose touches the ground.

- Return to starting position, and repeat.

- Do as many as you can in 1 set, working up to 3 sets.

Pull-ups

- Place your hands facing away from you on an assisted pull-up machine at a gym or on a pull-up bar.

- Engage your abs to keep your low back from swaying, and slowly pull yourself up so your chin reaches over the bar.

- Lower yourself slowly, and repeat (if you can!).

- Do as many as you can in 1 set, working up to 3 sets.

STRONGER Upper Body, Lungs, and Back

WHY. Improved flexibility in the upper spine—and in your chest muscles—can help improve lung capacity (breathe easier!), encourage better posture while running, and enhance muscle function in your core and lower body. Proper strength and mobility in the thoracic spine also prevents excess stress of the low back.

HOW

Thoracic spine mobilization

- Lie on the floor with feet flat on the ground and knees bent, resting your upper body on a 6-inch-diameter foam roller just below your neck, perpendicular to your body.

Support head in hands

- Interlock your fingers and place your hands at the top of your neck, supporting your head but allowing it to drop toward the floor as you roll.

- Moving your body by pushing with your feet, which are still flat on the floor, roll your upper body along the foam roller, stopping around the base of your rib cage. Roll back up to starting position.

- Repeat.

Pectoral stretch
- Lie with a foam roller lined up along your spine with your head resting on the roller, your feet flat on the ground, and your knees bent.

- Open your arms, palms up, and lay them along the floor as if to make a snow angel. Start with your arms at the top range of the snow angel.

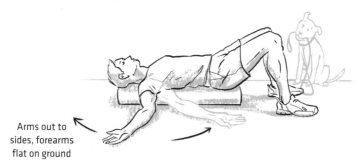

Arms out to
sides, forearms
flat on ground

- Slide your arms down toward your lower body, dragging your fingers (and eventually your forearms) along the floor.

- Stop at any particularly tight spots and take a few extra breaths.

- Return to starting position.

- Repeat.

STRONGER Body

WHY. Teaching your body's muscle groups to work together in a controlled strength exercise translates to maximum agility and efficiency on the trail.

HOW

Overhead squat

- Stand with your heels lined up underneath your shoulders and your toes pointing slightly out.

- Raise your arms over your head with thumbs pointing back, straight up from your shoulders in a Y position.

- While keeping your elbows locked and straight, squat down toward the ground, initiating from your hips as your trunk

---

Once you can keep your hands and forearms in contact with the ground through the full range of motion, your **flexibility** is good and normal. If you still can't do it after a month of trying, get some hands-on help. See "Practitioners," page 162.

leans forward. Then bend your knees to squat lower, keeping your back straight, knees driving out, chest and head up, and heels down.

- Return to starting position by first straightening your knees, then standing up straight from your hips.

- Repeat.

Keep back stright

If you can't lower to a **full squat**—thighs parallel to the floor—with your arms overhead, start by holding on to something for balance and work up to the over-head version.

RULE *of* **THUMB** For best results, do these exercises three times a week. (You can do the thoracic mobilization and pectoral stretch daily.)

Technically sound

Moving swiftly (or sometimes just staying upright) on trails of varying character and surface type—rock-strewn, root-riddled, twisty, or narrow—requires a bit of technique. And trails that head either up- or downhill are easier to manage with a few tips regarding body position and mental focus.

Best foot forward

Negotiating technical trails with ease calls for a combination of mental and physical prowess. But practice enough, and it becomes second nature.

technical \'tek-ni-kul l\ *adj.* 1. Tricky.

- **Stay relaxed.** Tensing up increases your chances of a misstep; also, a tense body can suffer more from a misstep than a loose body.

- **Look ahead.** Keep your gaze a few paces in front of you so that your body—and your mind—knows what's coming.

- **Look where you want to go.** Choose a line you want your feet to take. Follow that line with your feet.

- **Keep your hips under you.** Keeping your hips directly beneath you—and not sticking your rear end out behind you or excessively tucking your tailbone—helps maintain balance.

- **Place your feet flat.** Stepping down with a flat foot instead of on your heel gives you more surface area for landing and maintaining control with each step.

- **Widen your arm swing.** Swinging your arms in a slightly wider position (than when road running) will add balance to your body.

line \līn\ *n.* 1. The specific path you take on a trail.

good line \gŏod līn\ *n.* 1. Specific path you take that allows you to move quickly and with minimal effort. 2. *Hi, I'm Mark. What's your name?*

bad line \bad līn\ *n.* 1. Specific path you take that makes you slow down or fall down. 2. *If you were a fruit, you'd be a fineapple.*

 **THE DIRT** If a trail is rock-strewn to the right but smooth on the left, the left side is the better line if you want the path of least resistance. Some runners are very comfortable on technical terrain and may choose the harder line—in order to pass other trail users or simply for the challenge.

"If you hit a root when you're in good posture and your stride is underneath you, your center of gravity recovers. If your posture is lazy, you're more susceptible to a full-body yard sale on the trail. The good news is, typically, people have better form on a trail, even if they're not trying to. The changing terrain naturally shortens your stride, which keeps your hips and your feet underneath you."

GRANT ROBISON, New Balance Good Form Ambassador

HIP CHECK

Keeping your hips under you and your pelvis in a neutral position—not sticking your butt out or tucking it under—is the best way to assure good form and optimal balance. Here's a trick to check or realign your form:

- Before running, or any time midrun (either while you're running or during a quick stop), reach over your head and interlock your fingers.

- Stretch your palms toward the sky, fingers interlocked.

- Hold for a few seconds. This helps situate your hips/pelvis in a healthy position.

Running uphill

When trails are steep, breathing becomes harder, legs fatigue more quickly, and you tend to feel every painstaking step. A few mental and physical cues can help the hills feel less mighty and more manageable.

- **Stand tall.** Folding over at the hips and dropping your head to look at your feet compresses the air flow from your diaphragm and lungs to your nose and mouth. Try to maintain as flat a back as possible by staying in an upright position.

- **Quick feet.** Shortening your stride and taking quick steps help maintain efficiency on climbs. Short strides also help keep you in a more upright position.

- **Drive those arms.** Power and momentum comes from a strong arm swing, so pump away to help propel your lower body.

- **Walk.** There is no shame in walking up a steep trail. Walking, in fact, is sometimes the faster and more efficient way to get up a hill. (See "Everybody's Got a Mountain to Climb," page 220.)

- **Walk with purpose.** If you change your stride from a run to a walk, make each step powerful and purposeful, and continue to try to maintain an upright body position.

Everybody's got a mountain to climb

There are various approaches to body positioning and stride when climbing steep trails. Some runners prefer one way over the other, but most opt for a variety of the following, depending on the gradient of the hill.

	PROS	CONS
Keep running (albeit slowly)	Maintains momentum, physically and mentally	Can be slower than power hiking Keeps heart rate high, which adds to overall fatigue It's tough
Power walking, arms swinging	Maintains optimal airflow for hard-breathing effort Slows heart rate to save energy Arm swing adds momentum	Upper body doesn't get a break Takes more effort than walking with hands on hips or knees
Power walking, hands on hips	Maintains optimal airflow for hard-breathing effort Slows heart rate to save energy Gives arms and upper body a break	No upper-body momentum
Power walking, hands on knees	Ability to push knees with each step adds power Slows heart rate to save energy Gives arms a break Provides a stretch in the low back	Bent-over position compresses airflow Hunching can make back ache

All downhill from here

Downhill trails—whether smooth or technical—intimidate some and look like playgrounds to others. To master the downhill, focus on the following cues.

- **Chill out.** Staying relaxed is key to running well downhill. Embrace the terrain ahead to keep minimal tension in your body.

- **Keep those arms wide.** A wide arm swing adds balance, each arm countering weight shifts in your footing and body position.

- **Try a shorter stride.** Quick, frequent steps allow you to pick through technical terrain. And on smooth downhill trails, quick steps keep you from overextending hamstrings and pulling on hips.

- **Keep weight over your hips.** Resist the temptation to sit back on a downhill and put the brakes on with your quads. Keeping your weight over your hips keeps your momentum forward and muscles in your legs and core engaged to maintain control.

Training: Mix it up

So you want to get faster. Who doesn't? Maybe you have a race in your sights or a nonrace goal, such as a run up your local mountain in a certain time (or without stopping). Or maybe you want to be able to hang with one of your faster trail running friends.

INGREDIENTS:
1 PART SPEED WORK
2 PARTS HILL TRAINING
1 PART LSD
1 RECOVERY RUN
1 DAY OFF

DIRECTIONS:
MIX ALL TOGETHER IN SOME FASHION THAT
MAKES SENSE FOR YOUR RUNNING GOALS
AND YOUR BODY, BAKE.

Trail running workouts are similar to road running workouts in that a mix of speed work, hill training, and endurance training makes you faster and stronger. But training on trails adds the physical fortitude of negotiating technical terrain. And training on trails takes away much of the pounding from doing these same types of workouts on pavement or concrete, for which your body will thank you.

Here's what to mix into your routine.

Hills

Hills. Running hills, at any pace, makes you a stronger runner. If most of your trail runs are on flat or gently rolling terrain, add a few hilly trail runs to your week. No hills where you live? See "Out of Molehills," page 228. **HOW OFTEN?** At least once a week.

Hill repeats. Running hard uphill for anywhere from 30 seconds to 5 minutes at a time, and recovering as you walk or jog back down the hill, is a time-tested way to gain strength and power. Warm up by running slowly for 10 to 15 minutes before tackling hard efforts uphill, and be sure to allow yourself enough time to recover—to lower your heart and breath rate—between efforts. Start with 2 or 3 repeats, building up from there. **HOW OFTEN?** Every few weeks, depending on the difficulty of the climb/effort.

Hill time trials. Busting your butt and gutting up a sustained climb teaches you how to suffer—an invaluable trait if you are looking to race on trails. Warm up for at least 10 minutes by running slowly on flat to gradually inclining terrain before switching on your hard-effort gear to reach the top of a climb. Aim to maintain a steady pace, and don't be alarmed if your head feels like it's going to explode. **HOW OFTEN?** No more than once a week.

Downhills. Those who train fast on downhills come out ahead in races, and with minimally sore quadriceps. Consider busting a gut on the downhill portion of a trail after a warm-up of at least 10 to 15 minutes. **HOW OFTEN?** No more than once a week.

Downhill strides. Downhill strides on sections no longer than a football field, done at a high but controlled speed, build leg turnover and strength. Allow ample recovery between efforts. This can be done on a sustained downhill trail, like a downhill fartlek (see "Fartleks," page 224). Do 6 to 8 repetitions. **HOW OFTEN?** Every other week.

Up-and-overs. Combining a short uphill effort with a short down-hill effort trains muscle groups needed for both up- and downhill and helps with similar transitions during races. Start a hard effort 30 seconds to 1 minute below the top of a hill, and then run 30 seconds to 1 minute hard down the other side. Recover and repeat. Warm up for at least 15 minutes beforehand. **HOW OFTEN?** No more than once a week.

Speed

Fartleks. "Fartlek" is Swedish for "speed play." To do one, a runner increases speed for anywhere from 30 seconds to 6 minutes, slowing to a jog between efforts. If you don't wear a watch, measure your efforts by the natural terrain: *I'm going to go hard until that tree/rock/prairie-dog hole.* **HOW OFTEN?** No more than once a week.

Intervals. These sustained speed efforts, 2 to 5 minutes long with recovery in between, work your heart and lungs. After a warm-up of 10 to 20 minutes, run a set number of intervals at roughly your 5K race pace. **HOW OFTEN?** No more than once a week.

Tempo runs. Tempo runs, like hill time trials, are a sustained effort, but you don't need to do them on hills, and you shouldn't go so hard that you feel your heart beating through your throat. Warm up for 10 to 15 minutes by running slowly. Increase your speed to just below racing speed, and hold that pace for 20 or so minutes (build up to 60 minutes if you plan on racing a marathon distance or longer). **HOW OFTEN:** No more than once a week.

Progression run. Starting a run slowly and increasing your speed throughout trains your body to push when it is most tired. Start this run slower than your normal pace, and increase your pace by gradual increments until you hold a strong and steady pace through the end. **HOW OFTEN:** Once every other week, alternating with LSD (see "LSD," below).

Grass striders. Striders, where you ease into a controlled, fast effort for 40 to 50 yards before returning to a slower speed and recovery, teach your legs how to turn over quickly. A quick turnover makes for efficient running. Running striders on grass gives your body the benefit of the grass's springiness. And running striders barefoot on grass allows your feet to function naturally on a forgiving surface and can improve running form. **HOW OFTEN:** No more than once a week.

Track workouts. You probably didn't become a trail runner to spend time running around a rubber oval, but if you've got racing in your sights, track workouts will benefit your running. Short distances at varying speeds give you a good gauge of fitness and effort. Search running websites for workouts based on your goal race distance. **HOW OFTEN?** Not very.

Distance

LSD. Not to be confused with dropping acid, LSD means "long, slow distance." Doing an increasingly longer LSD run every week or two builds endurance, and the key to LSD runs is the *S*, not the *L* or the *D*. Aim to run quite a bit slower than your regular pace. You are looking to increase the time on your feet; don't get caught up in mileage. **HOW OFTEN:** Once every 1 or 2 weeks.

Technique

Technical sections. Practicing on a technical section of trail teaches you how to choose a line (See "Best Foot Forward," page 216). During your run, repeat any short technical sections, working on staying relaxed and keeping your hips underneath you as you pick your way through the rocks, roots, and ruts. **HOW OFTEN:** Whenever you want.

> **TIP** If you're training for a race, study the racecourse for information—such as elevation gains and profiles—and train on a local route that closely mimics that profile.

Recover

Recovery run. A recovery run is a slow, gentle-on-your-body way to work out lactic acid and mental fatigue from a hard workout the day, or days, before. Enjoy your recovery run. Run casually with a friend or on a particularly scenic trail. Minimize big hills. **HOW OFTEN:** Once or twice a week, depending on your other workouts.

Day(s) off. These are just as important as workouts. Take them when you need them. Eat and drink well. Rest well. Look forward to your next run.

Maintenance runs

Maintenance run. Also known as easy runs, these runs go at a pace that's casual and comfortable on terrain you enjoy. Maintenance runs are what you run on days you're not doing specific workouts or notably recovering. **HOW OFTEN:** Two or three per week.

SAYS WHO

"To be a good runner, there are two major keys. One is that you have to be fairly versatile. The other is that you have to enjoy the kind of running you're doing. Variety in training, terrain, and scenery helps with both."

VINCE SHERRY, head coach of Team Run Flagstaff and cofounder of the Run S.M.A.R.T. Project

THE DIRT Running a variety of trails and routes makes you a stronger runner. If you run the same route/trail over and over at the same speed, your body gets so used to that route that your speed and strength gains become minimal.

RULE of THUMB Don't try to cram all of the above workouts, recovery days, and rest days into a week or even two or three. Pick and choose your hard efforts based on your goals, and take care not to increase your mileage or intensity more than 20 percent per week to minimize the likelihood of injury.

OUT OF MOLEHILLS

If you live in a flat environment but have your sights set on a race or goal involving hills, you'll need to get creative.

Stadium stairs. Area high schools or colleges often have football stadiums, and those stadiums have stairs. Find out when you're allowed to run and power-hike up and down those stairs, and go at it.

Building stairs. Find the tallest building around with open access to its stairwell for a great strength workout. Seek out outdoor stairwells for a (deep, gasping) breath of fresh air.

Bridges. Bridges spanning rivers and other waterways almost always rise to the center point of the bridge and descend down the other side. These inclines might not mimic Pikes Peak, and they'll most likely be paved, but they may be a good bet for a sustained climb in an otherwise flat environment.

Gym equipment. Gyms have a range of mechanical contraptions that mimic climbing uphill, from setting a treadmill to a steep percentage to stepping on the StairMaster or the moving stairs of a ClimbMill. Machines might not be exciting but they can make you darn strong.

Listen to your body

Recovery needs are highly personal, and it's far better to listen to your body than to follow anyone else's guidelines on how much time is needed to recover from a workout.

- **Body aches after a hard workout but feels better the next day?** A recovery run might do you good.

- **A specific part of your body still aches the following day?** Take a day off, or crosstrain wisely. (See "Crosstraining for Trail Runners," below.) Keep an eye on it, and if pain persists, see a practitioner of some sort. (See "Practitioners," page 162.)

- **Dead tired the day after a workout?** Take a day off. Or five.

- **So sore you can barely walk the next day?** A very slow recovery run or crosstraining of some sort will encourage blood flow and keep your beat-up soft tissues from tightening and healing poorly.

Crosstraining for trail runners

There are all sorts of fun sports and activities out there. Some are the perfect counterbalance to trail running, allowing your lower-body muscles and joints to actively recover while working your upper body. Those activities include:

- Rock climbing
- Swimming
- Yoga
- Pilates
- Weight lifting (upper body only)
- Gardening
- Ping-Pong

Crosstraining gives your running muscles a break, but hard efforts will still leave you fatigued—an intense swim, for example, will deplete your energy level and require recovery time.

Other crosstraining activities actively use your lower body, and while they might not be as demanding on certain muscles and joints as trail running, you are still using many of the same muscles and joints. These activities can be a great way to stay fit during an injury or to mix things up in your running week. But they shouldn't be counted as days off. And only if you do them very lightly should they be considered active recovery days. Those activities include:

- Road or mountain biking
- Tennis, soccer, volleyball, or other ball sport
- Rowing
- Hip-hop clubbing
- Nordic skiing
- Hiking

CHAPTER 12

How, Part II: Trail Racing

NATURAL HIGH!

SNACKS

NEW FRIENDS

ADRENALINE RUSH!

START

Races are like a party: decorations (start and finish line), friends (other racers), dancing (well, running), music (your heartbeat and foot strike and sometimes a band or sound system), and postrace food and drink.

Know that not all trail races are ultramarathons; you'll find every distance from 1 mile to over 100 miles. And races don't require you to have shaved legs, fancy gear, or blinding speed.

Why enter a race?

Racing adds a fun and exciting new level to your running. The benefits are many, including:

- **Pushing yourself.** See what you're capable of. Go longer, run faster, place higher. Pushing yourself is good for you.

- **Discovering new trails.** Running a race lets you discover new trails or experience familiar ones in a new way.

- **Support.** Trail races usually have aid stations stocked with water, electrolytes, and fuel like gels, chews, and/or pretzels and cookies. What better way to run farther or harder than you have before than with someone handing you a snack and a sip every few miles? And should you need medical help for any reason, a race has you covered.

- **Meeting good people.** Trail races generally draw a hearty, friendly group of people who aren't afraid to get dirty. This makes for great camaraderie on the trails and fun postrace festivities.

- **Adding purpose.** Having a race on the horizon can give purpose to your running. Plus, it gives you an out: *I can't mow the lawn today because I had a superhard tempo run* *this morning. My race is in three weeks!* Or *I can't make it to the PTA meeting because I have to train for my race.*

- **Feeling inspired.** Crossing a finish line is an amazing (and addictive!) feeling. Races often make you want to do even better next time, which is a great kick in the pants to amp up training.

No comparison

If you've done some races on roads, know that your trail running race times will not match your road times. Trail terrain, even if it's flat, may be slower due to roots, rocks, or ruts (or all three) or simply because a softer trail surface makes your feet turn over more slowly than on pavement.

And if the course is hilly, crosses streams, or twists through a forest, forget about it. So don't compare road racing times with trail racing times.

Trail race distances

Trail races vary from quite short to ridiculously long. Courses can cover smooth, flat dirt or send you up and over a mountain (or eight) or through dense backwoods and swamps.

Less than 5K. Trail races as short as 1 mile exist. Some cater to those who like a good butt-kicking by sending them straight up a ski slope, while others are designed with the beginner in mind and are often run on flat, smooth, wide dirt.

5K, 10K, half-marathon. A multitude of trail races in the 5K (3.1-mile), 10K (6.2-mile) and half-marathon (13.1-mile) distance take place across the country. Following a road race training plan for the same distance is a start—but be sure to spend as much time as possible on trails, and add some trail-specific workouts (see "Training: Mix It Up," page 221).

Odd distance. There are more "odd-distance" trail races than road races simply because trails and loops on trails vary in distance. You may find a race that's 2.8 miles, 7.4 miles, or 18 miles long. These nontraditional distances add to the fun, casual, don't-bother-with-your-splits nature of trail racing.

Marathon. A trail marathon, like a road marathon, is 26.2 miles—unless, of course, it's not. Because of the diverse nature of trails, some trail marathons are "around" 26 miles long, give or take a mile or two.

Ultramarathon. The word "ultramarathon" applies to any race over the distance of a marathon (unless it's 28 miles long and called a "trail marathon"; see "Marathon," previous page). Typical ultra-marathon distances are 50K, 50 miles, 100K, or 100 miles. Some are even longer, and not all are entirely on trails.

50K. Fifty kilometers is 31.07 miles. These races are commonly chosen as a new ultrarunner's foray into long-distance running.

50 miles. Fifty miles is 50 miles, and that's a lot (although to some ultrarunners, a 50-miler is a short race).

100K. 100K is 62.14 miles. This race distance is stout in its own right and is often used as a stepping-stone to the 100-mile distance.

100 miles. The 100-mile distance is a classic ultrarunner's pride and joy. Those who compete in 100-mile races over hill, dale, high-mountain passes, or dense jungle terrain are part of a tough-as-nails club.

More than 100 miles. Races longer than 100 miles exist since, as humans, we always want to know what else is possible.

Trail race types

Trail races, like road races, generally involve a start and a finish. But there are a wide variety of race types to choose from. Want to run with a team? Experience a multiday adventure? Jump over a fire pit? Take your pick!

Stage race. A race that covers a certain distance in a day, then allows racers to sleep and eat before racing again the next day.

Some stage races pit competitors against each other as individuals; some have teams. Stage races vary from two days to longer than two weeks.

One-way race. Also called "point-to-point" races, these start in one location and end in another. A shuttle is often provided from the finish line back to the start.

Relay race. Trail relay races pit teams against each other, with each runner racing a portion or portions of a trail and trading off with his or her teammates.

Obstacle race. These races vary in distance and send competitors across or through obstacles such as fire pits, barbed wire, and freezing water. In between these obstacles, the running happens off road.

Burro race. Burro races, held in certain mountain towns of Colorado, celebrate the history of mining by pitting runners and their teammate—a burro—against other runners and their burros. Runners lead or are led by—and are not allowed to ride—the burro.

Ride and Tie. Two runners, one horse. One runner starts off on horseback while the other runner travels by foot. The rider ties the horse to a tree or post and starts running, and the runner teammate catches up, unties the horse, and rides on.

Trail festivals. Sometimes races of one distance coincide with races of other distances in a day- or weekend-long festival of trail

 For more on racing and running with **burros or horses**, see "Running with Horses or Burros," page 197.

running. Distances often include races meant to suit a range of runners, including those under 10 years old.

Destination races. Choosing a race in an intriguing location makes for a great reason to travel. Just make sure you pack all the items you'll need (See "What You Need on Race Day," page 243).

FOREIGN VERSIONS OF COMMON RACE TERMS

	GOOD LUCK	ON YOUR LEFT	GOOD JOB
French	Merde!	Pardon! Attention!	Bravo!
Spanish	¡Buena suerte! ¡Que vaya bien!	¡Venga, venga! Por la izquierda derecha! ¡Paso!	¡Buen trabajo! ¡Felicidades! ¡Gran carrera!
Australian	Good luck, mate!	Coming up, mate! Through, mate! #$%!@%, mate!	Good on ya, mate!
Japanese	がんばって Gannbatte!	左通りま Hidaritorimasu! Migitorimasu! Torimasu!	お疲れさまでした Otsukaresamadeshita!
Hawaiian	Aloha!	Aloha!	Aloha!

 It is considered **bad luck** to say Good luck at a race start in France.

Nonrace Races

If you don't want to sign up for an official race, there are other options for testing your mettle against yourself and others.

FKT. "FKT" stands for "fastest known time." Runners take on routes such as the John Muir Trail or the Grand Canyon Rim-to-Rim-to-Rim route in order to nab the FKT record. An FKT web site keeps track of records and makes the efforts official. (Runners must announce to the web site that they plan to attempt the record, then show proof via photos of clock times, trailhead signs, and the like.)

Ego apps. Personal device applications exist that allow runners to pit themselves against each other virtually whenever they want. Feel like throwing down on a 400-foot climb on your local trail, and want to see how you measure up against other runners in town? There's an app for that.

Choosing a Race

With so many distances and race types, how do you choose a race that's right for you? A few factors weigh in.

- **How far do you want to run?** Seeking out a race by its distance is a good place to start.

- **Where do you want to go?** Maybe there's a race being held on a trail network you've always wanted to check out or in a locale you've always wanted to visit.

- **Groupthink?** Getting a friend or group of friends together to sign up for, train, and maybe travel to a race together can be a great motivator and adds smack-talking fun and a supportive environment on race day.

- **How much does it cost?** Trail running races vary in price. If the entry fee is expensive, know that you likely won't regret doing it. And, there may be some cool race schwag included with the entry fee.

schwag \shwag\ *n.* 1. Also called "swag," which stands for "stuff we all get," it is given to registered trail racers and can be anything from a long-sleeved technical running shirt printed with a race logo to a potted plant to your race number and four safety pins.

> **TIP** Not prepared for your race? Roll with it. Sometimes even with the best intentions, your training is less than ideal. If you do jump into an event unprepared or at the last minute, have fun, and just remember to race conservatively so that you don't end up having to reread the "First Aid" chapter.

Early bird gets the race

Some races, popular ultramarathons in particular, sell out quickly. Be on the ball by choosing your race far enough ahead of time and following the proper sign-up protocols. And know that some races are hard to get into, whether they sell out or not.

Some require entrants to qualify via other races. Some want proof of completion of long-distance road races within a certain time. And others choose applicants via lottery. (Some allow begging.)

How to prepare

Once you've picked a race and signed up, it's time to prep.

Train. Training with some combination of training efforts (see "Training: Mix It Up," page 221) readies you for race day and gives purpose to your runs. Training smartly (not too much, not too little) makes you stronger and faster and will make race day hurt less.

Mimic the course. Check out the race's elevation profile, and, if feasible, train on terrain similar to what you'll face on race day.

Do a dress rehearsal, or three or four. Wear what you plan on wearing on race day, from your shoes and socks to your headwear and sunglasses. If anything chafes or otherwise annoys you, try something else.

Train with fuel. Your gut needs training, too. Hydrate and fuel during your workouts so your digestive system gets used to ingesting under stress. If something you ingest doesn't sit right with you, try something else.

Train with the race's fuel. Most races list what brands of hydration drink and fuel (such as gels and bars) they'll provide at aid stations. Train with those items to see if they work with your body. If they don't, carry your own fluids and fuel that you know don't upset your stomach.

What you need on race day

In addition to being healthy and ready with a good attitude, there are certain things that will make your race day more comfortable.

On your person

- **Proof of registration** to pick up bib number if you preregistered.

- **ID** to prove you're you.

- **Bib number** pinned to a layer of clothing that you will not shed when hot.

- **Safety pins,** usually found on the table where you got your bib number or in your schwag bag.

- **Pre-race clothes** to stay warm before the race (consider wearing something expendable that can be ditched at the start line).

- **Race attire.** Choose wisely, and know that it's okay to be a little cold at the starting line. You'll heat up soon enough during the race.

- **Race footwear.** Consider the terrain, the conditions, and the weight of your shoes. If you only own one pair of running shoes, then those are your perfect race shoes.

- **Sunglasses** are highly recommended on an exposed course. If the course takes place mostly in the woods or dips in and out of the shade, you may not want them.

- **Hat or visor** to shield eyes from the sun. But know that if the course ducks under low branches, hats/visors shield eyes from those, too.

- **Lightweight gloves** if it's cold, or if the course is technical and you may be grabbing tree trunks or scrambling over boulders.

- **Sustenance,** just enough to get you between aid stations. Most races have aid stations every few miles (some are farther apart than that). Most aid stations have water and an electrolyte replacement as well as fuel. Check the race web site or registration packet for details.

- **Ultrarace-specific accoutrements.** If you're racing an ultra, you'll likely have a whole slew of items on you such as salt tablets, extra gels, minor first aid, and maybe fresh socks—as compact and light as possible. (You'll likely also have a support crew to help resupply all of this during the race.)

In your car/bag

- **Water** to hydrate on your way to the race.

- **Fuel.** Pack what you plan to eat before the race and something quick and protein-rich to eat afterward. (See "Nutrition," page 82.)

- **Sunblock,** even on cloudy days. You don't need another thing (like burnt skin) hurting after the race.

- **Lip balm.** Lips get dry out there.

- **Postrace clothes.** You'll want to get out of sweaty, dirty clothes after the race or at least pull something on to stay warm while you enjoy postrace festivities.

- **Postrace shoes.** Swap your race shoes for comfy slip-ons, clean running shoes, or flip-flops.

- **Postrace socks.** A fresh pair of socks can feel like heaven after a dirty race. Consider compression socks if you want to aid recovery.

- **Money** for postrace food, beverage, or the CD of the band playing at the postrace party.

- **Credit card and health insurance card.** You likely won't need either, but better safe than sorry.

Race tactics

There's definitely a lot of fun and excitement in starting a race having no idea where it will go, what the course looks like, or what you will encounter and when. However, if your goal is to race your best, a little planning and some strategy will help you run the smartest, fastest race you can.

Study the course map. Knowing details about the course—that once the trail takes a hard left, the climbing is over, for example—can help you plan your pacing.

Ask for beta. Being told by a race veteran that the stairs are slippery and to take the dirt path instead can be invaluable midrace.

Be aware of bottlenecks. Knowing ahead of time that the race starts on a wide trail and quickly heads into 5 miles of singletrack (read: hard to pass) may be invaluable. Consider using this beta by starting faster than normal to avoid being stuck behind folks slower than you for 5 miles.

The word "beta" is a term originally shortened from "Betamax," as rock climbers used to view Betamax videocassettes to see how a climb was done before trying it themselves. Nowadays, the term is used to mean any knowledge gained ahead of an event or endeavor.

Know how to pass. If you want to pass on a singletrack, do your best to pass without making other competitors move over, even if it means running through brush for a few yards before regaining the trail in front of them. Say something like *If there's room, can I get by you?* Or *On your left, when you can.* But don't expect them to stop their race to move out of your way.

Know how to be passed. If you have a runner on your heels who is anxious to get by, do your best to move to the side when it makes sense. Say something like *Do you want to go by?* to make sure they're ready to pass.

Be pleasant. When you're passing, being passed, or just running next to someone, be pleasant. Saying, *Good job!* or *Go get 'em!* adds to a good race atmosphere.

Fuel early and often. Don't get so caught up in the race that you forget to eat or drink. Staying on top of fueling and hydration will help you avoid bonking (see "Nutrition," page 82), something you don't want to do on race day.

TIP To shed a lightweight jacket midrace without slowing down, unzip to the bottom of the zipper (but not entirely), slide your arms out, and tie the sleeves around your waist. Bunching and rolling the body of the jacket helps keep the excess out of your way. This works even while wearing a pack—you don't have to remove the pack. You may look a little like Pigpen from the Peanuts gang, but you'll be fast Pigpen.

Recover

Race efforts take more out of you—physically and mentally—than do training runs, even hard training runs. Give yourself ample time to recover.

- Get a massage. (See "Practitioners," page 162.)
- Enjoy your new friends. (See "Running with Human or Animal Friends," page 186.)
- Use your self-care tools. (See "Self-Care," page 163.)
- Take a recovery run. (See "Training: Mix It Up," page 221.)
- Take a break from running and crosstrain. (See "Crosstraining for Trail Runners," page 229.)
- Eat and drink well. (See "Nutrition," page 82.)
- Take time off if you need it, want to, and will mentally and physically benefit from it. (See "Day(s) Off," page 226.)

If you raced, any distance, any type of course, congratulations. Be proud.

And if you didn't race but enjoy your nonracing miles on trails, congratulations. Be proud.

You're a trail runner.

Acknowledgments

Thank you to all the people whose input helped shape this book.

To illustrator Charlie Layton for elevating my goofy pencil sketches and transforming them into professional, way-better drawings; to editor Casey Blaine of VeloPress for smart edits and giving me the go-ahead for the book in the first place; to Vicki Hopewell for her great design work; to Connie Oehring for her sharp grammar.

To physical therapist and friend Charlie Merrill for his knowledge of the athlete's working body and how to constantly improve upon it. To Vince Sherry on all things training. To Sunny Blende and her nutritional knowledge. To Tod Schimelpfenig and his wilderness medicine expertise. To Kate Wilmot and her animal safety experience.

To Grant Robison for his running form prowess and John Vonhof for sharing his foot-care methods. To Daniel Ferris, PhD, and Dean Hebert for their scientific wisdom. To Deena Kastor and

Henry Guzman for their support. To Allison Heaney for her veterinary expertise and Leo Lloyd for his lightning safety advice.

To Russ Kiernan for his ride and tie wisdom and Brian Metzler for sharing his burro running experiences (and for so much else). To Nicolas Mermoud, Tetsuro Ogata, Emma Roca, and Rod Judd for their language. To Darcy Piceu, Maia Tozzi, and Sara Yoder for letting me bounce stuff off them while we ran. And to the legendary Jack "Dipsea Demon" Kirk, who replied to my letter 15 years ago, leading to my first feature story about trail running.

To my book-writing mom, Paula; athletic and competitive dad, Larry; and sharp-witted sister, Kelley, for their support.

To my sons—Sam, thoughtful and creative, who told me he liked my illustration drafts while he did his homework next to me, and Ben, who inspires me with his smarts and because he's just plain funny.

To my dog, Hannah, with whom I shared many happy running trails.

To my husband, Mark Eller, who read everything even when he didn't feel like it, offering great edits and insights and calming me the f*** down at times.

And to all the people with whom I've ever shared a trail—you all influenced this book in one way or another.

Index

About the Author and Illustrator

Lisa Jhung is a freelance journalist based in Boulder, Colorado. She's a contributing editor for *Runner's World* and edits the runnersworld .com/trail running website. Lisa writes about the sports she loves (and the gear that goes with them) for many national magazines. Her work has appeared in *Backpacker*, *Competitor*, *Cosmo*, *DETAILS*, *Fitness*, *Inside Triathlon*, *Men's Journal*, *Mental Floss*, *Outside*, *Outside Buyer's Guide*, *Runner's World*, *Running Times*, *SHAPE*, *Trail Runner*, *Triathlete*, *Women's Running*, and more. Lisa has also served as an editor at *Trail Runner* and a co-founding editor of *Adventure Sports Magazine*.

Lisa ran her first 5K at age 8 but started running regularly after realizing that hiding behind the high-jump mats during high school track practice wasn't going to help her run the timed mile needed to walk onto her college volleyball team. Her first trails were the beaches of San Diego, California, and, after she figured out that sitting on the bench during volleyball games wasn't much fun, the bluff trails of Santa Barbara. A couple of decades, hundreds of trail races, triathlons, and adventure races—from three hours to seven days long—later, she's still running and is still a sucker for anything with a finish line.

Lisa lives with her husband, Mark Eller, and two boys, Sam and Ben.

Charlie Layton is an illustrator and designer based in Philadelphia. His clients run the gamut from book publishers to toy manufacturers to roller derby teams. In his spare time, he enjoys mountain biking, snowboarding, and rock climbing.